THE PROHIBITION ERA IN AMERICAN HISTORY

Suzanne Lieurance

Enslow Publishers, Inc.

40 Industrial Road	PO Box 38
Box 398	Aldershot
Berkeley Heights, NJ 07922	Hants GU12 6BP
USA	UK

http://www.enslow.com

Library of Congress Cataloging-in-Publication Data

Lieurance, Suzanne.
  The Prohibition Era in American history / Suzanne Lieurance.
      p. cm. — (In American history)
  Summary: Explores the impact on American society and history of the
  Eighteenth Amendment and the Volstead Act, which prohibited any use of
  alcohol except for religious or medicinal purposes.
  Includes bibliographical references and index.
  ISBN 0-7660-1840-7
  1. Prohibition—United States—History—Juvenile literature. [1.
  Prohibition. 2. United States—History—1919–1933. 3. United
  States—Social life and customs—1918-1945.] I. Title. II. Series.
  HV5089 .L655 2002
  363.4'1'0973—dc21
                                              2002004280

Printed in the United States of America

10 9 8 7 6 5 4 3 2 1

To Our Readers:
We have done our best to make sure all Internet Addresses in this book were active
and appropriate when we went to press. However, the author and the publisher
have no control over and assume no liability for the material available on those
Internet sites or on other Web sites they may link to. Any comments or
suggestions can be sent by e-mail to comments@enslow.com or to the address on
the back cover.

Illustration Credits: Courtesy Library of Congress, reproduced from
the *Dictionary of American Portraits*, published by Dover Publications,
Inc., in 1967, p. 97; Painting by Gilbert Stuart, reproduced from the
Dictionary of American Portraits, published by Dover Publications, Inc.,
in 1967, p. 22; Records of the Redpath Chautauqua Collection, Special
Collections Department, University of Iowa Libraries, Iowa City, Iowa,
p. 48; Reproduced from the Collections of the Library of Congress,
pp. 15, 53, 55, 57, 63, 73, 86; Westerville Public Library, pp. 6, 10, 12,
27, 29, 40, 43, 45, 46, 49, 52, 60, 61, 67.

Cover Illustration: National Archives and Records Administration;
Reproduced from the Collections of the Library of Congress; Westerville
Public Library.

★ CONTENTS ★

AMERICA SAYS "NO" TO ALCOHOL

The year was 1920. For the past thirty years many people in the United States had been moving from the country to the city. There were more jobs in the cities. People went there to find work. Great numbers of people had been immigrating to the United States for many years, too. This huge increase in population brought about many social changes. Among those changes were more crime, poverty, and violence.

Many Americans felt that alcohol was at the root of all these problems. They wanted the sale of alcohol to be outlawed or prohibited, thinking that this would be a solution.

Three years before, in August 1917, the Senate had voted 65 to 20 in favor of creating the Eighteenth Amendment. This amendment would prohibit manufacture, sale, and transportation of alcohol. In December of that year, the House of Representatives had voted 282 to 124 in favor of Prohibition, too. Congress had then sent this proposed amendment to

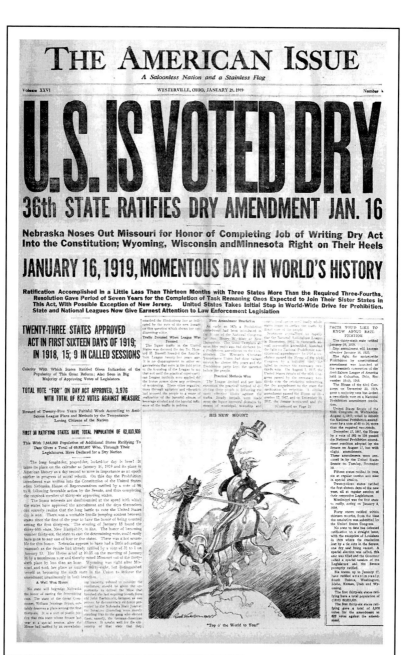

Newspapers across the country proclaimed the start of the Prohibition era.

the states for ratification, or approval. Three fourths of the states would have to approve the amendment before it became law.

According to the amendment, the states had a time limit of seven years to ratify it. If the amendment were not ratified within this time, it would not be added to the Constitution. It did not take that long for ratification, however. By January 16, 1919, thirty-six (three fourths) of the forty-eight states had approved the amendment. (Alaska and Hawaii had not yet become states.) Only Connecticut and Rhode Island never ratified the amendment.

The Eighteenth Amendment

The Eighteenth Amendment would outlaw the manufacture, sale, and transportation of intoxicating liquors within the United States and its territories. It would become effective on January 16, 1920. This was one year after ratification.

Alcohol would not be banned entirely under this new amendment. Churches and synagogues would still be able to use wine for sacraments. Alcohol would still be sold for medicinal purposes. Back then, alcohol was used as a general tonic, believed to promote good health. Alcohol was also often prescribed to treat toothaches and other common ailments, just as some medicines that contain alcohol are used today.

Americans who had liquor at home could drink it there, too. They could not buy or make any more

Section 1.

AFTER ONE YEAR FROM THE RATIFICATION OF THIS ARTICLE THE MANUFACTURE, SALE, OR TRANSPORTATION OF INTOXICATING LIQUORS WITHIN, THE IMPORTATION THEREOF INTO, OR THE EXPORTATION THEREOF FROM THE UNITED STATES AND ALL TERRITORY SUBJECT TO THE JURISDICTION THEREOF FOR BEVERAGE PURPOSES IS HEREBY PROHIBITED.

Section 2.

THE CONGRESS AND THE SEVERAL STATES SHALL HAVE CONCURRENT POWER TO ENFORCE THIS ARTICLE BY APPROPRIATE LEGISLATION.

Section 3.

THIS ARTICLE SHALL BE INOPERATIVE UNLESS IT SHALL HAVE BEEN RATIFIED AS AN AMENDMENT TO THE CONSTITUTION BY THE LEGISLATURES OF THE SEVERAL STATES, AS PROVIDED IN THE CONSTITUTION, WITHIN SEVEN YEARS FROM THE DATE OF THE SUBMISSION HEREOF TO THE STATES BY THE CONGRESS.[1]

The Eighteenth Amendment prohibited people of the United States from making, selling, transporting, importing, or exporting alcoholic beverages. It also gave Congress the power to use the government's agencies to enforce the law.

once that was gone, however. Many people did not understand this. They thought that, according to the new law, they could still store liquor in places other than their homes. Since Americans did not know when they would be able to purchase alcohol again, many people stored liquor in commercial warehouses and safe deposit vaults. Soon they were in for a big surprise. Just one day before the start of Prohibition, a federal judge declared that all liquor not in a person's home after January 16 could be taken away. When people heard this, they rushed to move their personal supplies of alcohol to their homes. They had to get it there before midnight on January 16, 1920.

Funerals and Celebrations

At one minute past midnight on Friday, January 16, 1920, many people across the country celebrated. Mock funerals were held in nightclubs and hotels. Popular songs of the times, such as "Good-by Forever," were played by bands at elegant hotels. Other bands played composer Frederic Chopin's "Funeral March" to signal an end to legalized alcohol use.

The Anti-Saloon League of New York was an organization in favor of the prohibition of alcohol. The league said, "IT is here at last—dry [without alcohol] America's first birthday . . . The Anti-Saloon League wishes every man, woman and child a happy New Dry Year."[2]

Church bells rang out across the country. Parades, meetings, and prayer services were conducted in many

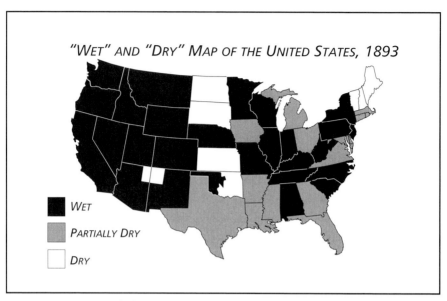

In 1893, most of the United States was "wet," meaning alcohol was allowed. However, about 38 percent of the states were at least partially dry, and six states were completely dry.

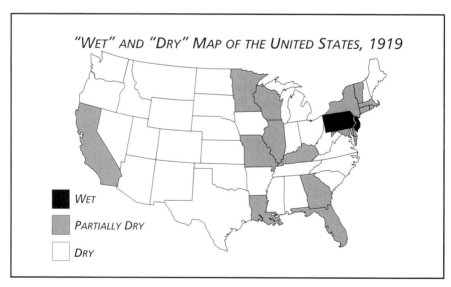

By January 1, 1919, fifteen days before the Eighteenth Amendment was ratified, only two states were still completely wet. Sixteen states were partially dry, and thirty states were completly dry.

towns. One of the biggest celebrations took place in Norfolk, Virginia. A mock funeral was held for John Barleycorn. Barleycorn was an imaginary man. He was the symbol of all the evils of alcohol. Many people were happy to see him finally put to rest.

A coffin containing a life-size rag doll named John Barleycorn was paraded through the streets. A man in a devil costume danced around the coffin. He seemed to be mourning a dear, departed friend.

Ten thousand people in favor of prohibiting the sale of alcohol gathered for Barleycorn's funeral service. It was led by an ex-baseball player named Billy Sunday who was now a popular preacher. Reverend Sunday had campaigned against drinking for many years. As the service began, Sunday stood before the coffin. "Good-bye, John," he said. "You were God's worst enemy. You were hell's best friend."[3]

A headline in *The New York Times* on January 17 reported that, "John Barleycorn Died Peacefully at . . . The Toll of 12."[4]

While these celebrations took place, other people were unhappy about Prohibition. People who owned breweries, distilleries, and wineries had to figure out some other way to make a living. People with jobs in bottling, packaging, selling, and delivering alcoholic beverages needed to find new jobs. Some people simply did not want to give up alcohol. This was definitely not a time of celebration for them.

John Barleycorn Is Dead!

||||||||||||||||||||||||||||||||||||||||||||||||||||||||||||||||||||||||||||||||||||||||||||||||||||||||||||||

A Memorial Will be Held for Him in the
Presbyterian Church

Friday Evening, January 16th

At 7:30

FIVE MINUTE tributes to the "departed" will be made by the following persons:

The Distiller, to be impersonated by	Geo. L. Stoughton
The Brewer, to be impersonated by	Dr. Albert E. Porter
The Landlord, to be impersonated by	H. B. Sowers
The Undertaker, to be impersonated by	Prof. E. L. Baxter
The Policeman, to be impersonated by	Rev. H. A. Smith
The Drunkard, to be impersonated by	C. S. Pilkington
The Drunkard's wife, to be impersonated by	Mrs. C. S. Pilkington
The Wet Editor, to be impersonated by	J. H. Larimore
The Wet Politician, to be impersonated by	Dr. T. M. Hare
The Saloon Keeper, to be impersonated by	Rev. Chas. H. Sowers
The Saloon Keeper's wife, to be impersonated by	Mrs. S. W. Keister
Pres. Ohio Home Rule Association, to be impersonated by	Prof. R. H. Wagoner
Anarchist, to be impersonated by	Rev. Milo G. Kelser
German—American Alliance adherent, to be impersonated by	T. H. Bradrick
Tax Objector, to be impersonated by	Prof. Chas. Snavely
Criminal, to be impersonated by	Prof. C. A. Fritz
The Wet Preacher, to be impersonated by	Dr. E. A. Jones
The summing up of mankind's verdict, and the final "farewell" words—	Dr. A. M. Courtenay

The program will be interspersed by appropriate music, under the direction of Prof. J. A. Bendinger.

Everybody is Invited   All Are Welcome
Free of Course

After the passage of the Eighteenth Amendment, funerals for the fictional John Barleycorn, who symbolized liquor, were held throughout the country.

The Volstead Act

After the Eighteenth Amendment took effect, the National Prohibition Act was created. The act was made so that people could understand the rules for the amendment. This act was designed to explain exactly what could and could not be done with alcoholic beverages. It also explained what the penalties would be for those people who broke the law.

The National Prohibition Act became known as the Volstead Act. It was named after Andrew Joseph Volstead, the Republican congressman from Minnesota who introduced the act in the House of Representatives. Volstead did not write this document, however. Wayne Wheeler of the Anti-Saloon League was the author of the Volstead Act. He gave it to Volstead to present to Congress. It passed in both houses of Congress, the House of Representatives and the Senate, in October 1919.

President Woodrow Wilson opposed Prohibition, but he tried to remain neutral to the Eighteenth Amendment. He could not be neutral to the Volstead Act, however. On October 27, he vetoed it. Many people in favor of Prohibition had used World War I as a reason for supporting Prohibition. They said that grain used for liquor should be saved to make bread during these hard times. President Wilson felt this was no longer a good reason to push for Prohibition. He was in favor of a temperance education program. It would teach people to drink responsibly. Wilson also felt that Prohibition should be a matter for local, not federal,

SOURCE DOCUMENT

To prohibit intoxicating beverages, and to regulate the manufacture production, use, and sale of high-proof spirits for other than beverage purposes, and to insure an ample supply of alcohol and promote its use in scientific research and in the development of fuel, dye, and other lawful industries.[5]

At the beginning of the National Prohibition Act (also called the Volstead Act), the law's purpose was clearly stated. Some people thought, however, that the law itself was needlessly complicated.

government. Congress did not agree. It overrode his veto. That meant that two thirds of the members of each house of Congress voted for the Volstead Act.

The Eighteenth Amendment was just three paragraphs long. The Volstead Act was much longer. It was also much more complicated. Part of it stated that any person who made or sold liquor would be fined no more than one thousand dollars or imprisoned no more than six months for the first offense. For the second offense, they would be fined not less than two hundred dollars, but not more than two thousand dollars, and they would be put in prison no less than one month, but not more than five years.[6]

Politicians and other government officials were serious about enforcing the Volstead Act. A Prohibition Unit was created. John F. Kramer was named commissioner of its headquarters. He declared:

This law will be obeyed in cities large and small, and in villages, and where it is not obeyed it will be enforced . . . We shall see to it that [liquor] is not manufactured nor sold nor given away nor hauled in anything on the surface of the earth or under the earth or in the air.[7]

The Volstead Act was doomed to fail for many complex reasons. A law such as this one should be short and clear. It should be easy to read and understand by anyone it might affect. It should not contain provisions that could cause different treatment for the rich and poor, or make it complicated or difficult to enforce. The law's penalties should be designed to prevent people from breaking it.

Part of the reason the Volstead Act failed was because it was not clear and easy to understand. It was confusing and complicated. It contained sixty-seven sections. Six more were added by a

President Woodrow Wilson vetoed the Volstead Act. Instead, he was in favor of using education to teach people the dangers of alcohol.

supplemental act. This made a total of seventy-three sections.

Police, attorneys, and judges of lower courts all interpreted the Volstead Act differently. It took the Supreme Court to decide the meaning of many of the act's provisions. People became confused about this law. Eventually, they did not pay much attention to the act. Later, they were even angry about it.

When President Warren Harding took office in 1921, he tried to make sure that the Volstead Act was enforced. He appointed Mabel Willebrandt, assistant attorney general, to be in charge of Prohibition enforcement, tax prosecutions, and federal prisons. Part of Willebrandt's job would be to assign federal raiding parties to arrest people who disobeyed the Volstead Act. Her job would turn out to be almost impossible.

Prohibition would not end America's problems. Instead, when the Eighteenth Amendment went into effect in 1920, it created a whole new set of problems that would trouble the nation for the next thirteen years.

The American Indians were familiar with alcoholic beverages long before the first pilgrims arrived from Europe. They made alcoholic drinks from corn and maple syrup. They would leave unripe corn in pools of water for several months. This would produce a mixture that was somewhat alcoholic.

Sometimes American Indians also drank the juices of various wild fruits and berries that had fermented (became alcoholic) naturally. American

THE HISTORY OF ALCOHOL AND THE BREWING INDUSTRY

Indians made another strong alcoholic beverage from the fruit of the pitahaya, a giant cactus. Unlike distilled liquors, these naturally fermented drinks probably did not have a high percentage of alcohol.

Alcohol in Early America

When the first English colonists came to America in the 1600s, they brought alcoholic beverages right along with them. These kinds of drinks made good sense back then. It was difficult to keep fresh drinking water aboard ship for long periods of time. Beer helped solve this problem. It became a common beverage for sea travelers. In his journal, one sailor offered the following advice for other travelers: "I would recommend to you to carry out a quantity of Molosses [sic] . . . in order to brew Beer with, for your daily drink, when your *Water becomes bad*."[1]

Settlers established the first permanent British settlement in Jamestown, Virginia, in 1607. Alcohol, which they called aqua vitae, was part of each colonist's supplies. Later, even the Puritans who sailed to America to settle the Massachusetts Bay Colony in 1630 brought alcohol with them. This included 12 gallons of distilled spirits, 10,000 gallons of beer, and 120 hogsheads of brewing malt.[2] When these supplies were used up, settlers started making more.

Although many early Americans drank alcohol, some attempts were made to prevent excessive drinking as early as 1633. At that time, Plymouth Colony prohibited the sale of spirits "more than 2 pence worth to anyone but strangers just arrived," according to author Ernest H. Cherrington.[3]

Popular Beverages

Once Europeans were settled in America, alcoholic drinks stayed popular for many reasons. Often water was difficult to get, unfit to drink, or it was not available. When settlers could get water, it was usually muddy or strange tasting since the only way to obtain it was from lakes, streams, rain, or deep wells. And, there was no way to purify it as we do today.

Bottled fruit juices and soft drinks were not around during colonial times. Milk spoiled quickly because there was no way to keep it cold. Coffee and tea cost a lot because they had to be imported. But alcoholic beverages like wine, beer, rum, hard cider, and whiskey were easy to produce. They did not spoil quickly, and they did not cost much, either. Whiskey became the most popular beverage. In the 1820s, whiskey cost just twenty-five cents per gallon.[4]

Alcohol's Role

In colonial days, doctors felt that alcoholic beverages were needed to help people stay healthy. They thought alcohol could cure all sorts of illnesses and injuries. Liquor was prescribed for almost every illness—from babies' teething pain to the aches and pains of old age. It was also believed that spirits (alcoholic beverages) helped to keep up a person's strength.

Part of many workers' wages was paid in alcohol. It was customary for workers to receive daily rations of rum or whiskey from their employer.

Rum and wine were served at weddings and funerals. Liquor was an important beverage at many community events.

Many people even built their own private breweries. In fact, William Penn, who Pennsylvania is named after, built his own brewery in Philadelphia, and George Washington built a brewery at Mount Vernon.

Thomas Jefferson did not like the use of strong liquor, called "ardent spirits," but he drank wine and served it often to guests during his two terms as president. At one time, Benjamin Franklin convinced a chaplain to give out a bit of rum after prayers to get soldiers to attend his services. Franklin noted, "And never were prayers more generally and more punctually attended."[5]

Liquor was used to trade. It served as money. Colonial traders exchanged brandy for beaver pelts with the American Indians and other traders. Early traders bartered cheap rum for valuable otter furs. This had terrible consequences. Some American Indian tribes became so addicted to alcohol that they lost most of their interest in trapping animals.

At first, American Indians did not know how to make distilled liquor like rum or whiskey. They were also afraid of it. They felt it was poison. They considered drunkenness to be disgraceful. Eventually, younger members of the tribes bartered with the traders for distilled liquor. John Le Blanc, an Ottawa Indian leader, after his first drink, was asked what he thought it contained. "Hearts and tongues," he said, "for when I have drunken plentifully of it, my heart is a thousand strong, and I can talk, too, with astonishing freedom and rapidity."[6]

Early Distilleries

As the colonies grew and became a nation, the demand for alcohol grew right along with them. As a result, many commercial distilleries opened. By 1792, there were 2,579 registered distilleries in the United States.[7]

Americans also began to produce whiskey in the mountains of western Pennsylvania, Maryland, and North Carolina. Farmers who grew rye, barley, and corn in these regions figured out that it was easier and cheaper to turn these grains into whiskey than it was to carry them over rough mountain roads to sell them.

The Whiskey Rebellion

The Revolutionary War (1775–1783) was a war between the American colonies and England, which led to the creation of the United States. After this war, the new American government decided to use liquor as a way to raise money. A tax was placed on rum and molasses (used to make rum) that were imported from other countries. American-made whiskey was also taxed.

Times were tough for many farmers who were trying to recover from the Revolution. This tax upset them. They also thought the government was trying to keep them from drinking hard liquor, and that was none of the government's business. "If any man supposes that a mere law can turn the taste of a people from ardent spirits," said Congressman Fisher Ames of Massachusetts, "he has a romantic notion of legislative power."[8]

In 1794, the tax on whiskey created a serious revolt among the farmers. This revolt was called the Whiskey Rebellion. Farmers refused to pay the tax collectors.

President George Washington sent troops to put down the Whiskey Rebellion, which occurred because some farmers felt a tax on whiskey was unfair.

Fighting broke out. President Washington decided to step in. He sent about fifteen thousand soldiers to western Pennsylvania to end the rebellion.[9]

More Distilleries Open

During the eighteenth century, Americans were brewing beer and producing hard cider. Many were also distilling hard liquors such as applejack, peach brandy, and corn and rye whiskey. Alcohol was a regular part of the American diet.

Alcohol was usually served at home. People drank with meals and on breaks from their work. Farm workers, sailors, and soldiers were given a daily ration of rum or whiskey. Most everyone enjoyed alcohol. Even clergymen drank. Often, they would be offered alcoholic refreshments as they made visits to the homes of people in their congregation. This could amount to several drinks a day.

By 1810, the number of distilleries had increased to 14,191. These distilleries produced about 25 million gallons of ardent spirits. Some 8 million gallons were imported and about 134,000 gallons were exported. The total ardent spirits produced and imported was about 33 million gallons.[10] This brought the average use per person to almost 4.5 gallons per year for every man, woman, and child in the country. This did not even include all the spirits produced in private stills at people's homes.[11]

Drinking Habits Change

Americans' drinking habits began to change. According to the historian W. J. Rorabaugh (a leading authority on American drinking habits in the nineteenth century), the 1820s saw a shift to more frequent binge drinking.[12] Binge drinking meant people were drinking a lot at one time, both alone and with friends or family. Americans, especially white men, drank hard liquor to the point of drunkenness more and more. Rorabaugh thought this was due to rapid economic and social change. People were working more in larger factories. Before 1810, a worker in a small shop could hope that, before too many years passed, he would own his own shop. Now, the chance of owning a factory was not as likely. Drinking became a way for workers to drown their sorrows or stay content with their limited opportunities.

In the mid-1800s, Americans' drinking habits changed again. Some people still drank too much, but more and more people became concerned about the effects of alcohol. As a result, fewer people drank and more and more temperance groups formed.

Immigrants and a War

Around 1840, America began to experience a great wave of new immigrants. Most of them came from Germany and Ireland. Most of these people were poor, unskilled, and uneducated. They became part of the lowest class of American society. Drinking was an acceptable and normal everyday part of their native cultures. However, in America their drinking habits became symbolic of their lower-class status.

By the time these new immigrants arrived, the descendants of earlier immigrants had become established in America. Many of them were now the country's middle class. Part of their objection to drinking was the association it had with the lower class. People who did not believe in drinking were ready to do more than just try to persuade drinkers to give up alcohol. They decided it was time to get rid of the alcohol itself. However, the Civil War started in 1861 because of a dispute between the Northern and Southern states over slavery and states' rights. People became more concerned with the war than they were with drinking. People also used drinking as a way to deal with the problems the war created. For many years, there were few restrictions placed on the manufacture or sale of alcoholic beverages.

After the War

After the Civil War ended in 1865, the population increased quickly. The brewing (beer) industry became the most prosperous of the alcohol-beverage industries at that time.

German immigrants had introduced lager beer to the United States, too. It became very popular. By 1890, beer was the main alcoholic drink in the American market.

Many technological changes influenced the way Americans drank. New advances such as the railroad, the telegraph, and mechanical refrigeration made it possible for brewing to become big business. A few brewers were able to build big companies that could produce large amounts of beer. They could sell their products in both national and international markets.[13]

Saloons

By the early 1800s, America was in the middle of a second great wave of new immigrants. This time, people came mainly from southern and eastern Europe. There were Jews from Russia, Romania, and Poland; Catholics from Ireland; and other groups from Hungary and Germany. Like the earlier wave of immigrants in the 1840s, these people were mostly poor, unskilled, and uneducated. And, once again, they became part of the lower class. Middle-class America was still composed of mostly whites of Protestant, Anglo-Saxon origin.

The lower class liked to drink in saloons. Saloons were businesses that sold liquor by the glass to be drunk there. Breweries wanted to increase sales, so they would often help people start saloons that sold their products. Breweries would loan money to potential saloonkeepers and even provide signs and other advertising to help saloonkeepers get set up. To try to sell more and more beer, breweries helped more and more people become saloon owners.

According to Larry Engelmann, author of *Intemperance, the Lost War Against Liquor*, by the early 1900s, there were more saloons in America than churches, schools, hospitals, libraries, jails, theaters, or parks.[14]

In 1905, a man named John M. Barker wrote a book called *The Saloon Problem and Social Reform*. Barker felt the saloon was the major producer of crimes and criminals. Saloons often played an important role in the community, however. In a small coal-mining town such as Westville, Illinois, one resident said the saloon "is the only decent place we fellows have to go. We have a newspaper to read, another fellow to argue with, and we can put our feet on the table and eat all the free lunch we want."[15]

In 1907, a man named George Kibbe Turner wrote an article for the April issue of *McClure's Magazine*. The article was about the city of Chicago and the alcohol business there. In his article Turner said,

> Chicago has four times as many saloons as it should have, from any standpoint whatever, except, of course,

The Full Father and

The empty stocking.

—(The Instructor.)

Thirty-Six States Can Change This
By Constitutional Amendment

SERIES G. No. 17.

THE AMERICAN ISSUE PUBLISHING CO.,
Westerville, Ohio.

Many critics saw saloons as places where men wasted away the hours drinking while their neglected children remained at home. In this poster, a girl has missed her Christmas because her father is spending his money at the local saloon.

the brewers' and the wholesalers' . . . The Chicago market is thoroughly saturated with beer, and incidentally with other liquor. Reckoning it out by population, every man, woman, and child in Chicago drank, in 1906, two and one-quarter barrels of beer—that is, seventy gallons,—three and one-half times the average consumption in the United States. . . .[16]

Chicago was not the only city with a lot of saloons. There were saloons all across the country. According to Engelmann, by 1909, there was one licensed saloon for every three hundred people in America.[17]

With so much competition, each saloonkeeper had to figure out ways to get customers to enter his saloon instead of someone else's. Then, he had to get these customers to drink more. One way many saloonkeepers did this was to provide the customer with a free lunch.

Some people did not like saloons. According to Norman H. Clark in his book *Deliver Us From Evil*, to these people, saloons were places "where the fathers of young children floated away a week's wages that could have gone to food, clothing and education."[18]

Life was not easy for the average working man. Saloons provided a place where overworked men could go to forget about the problems of the workplace. Some thought this made organization of workingmen more difficult. In the late 1800s and early 1900s, the unions had very little power. Without strong unions, there was no successful way to complain about problems on the job, or try to get better working conditions. After a few drinks, though, a worker's problems did not seem so bad. Tom Lewis, president

YOUR DAUGHTER OR THE SALOONKEEPER'S— WHICH?

When the writer spoke to the men in the Michigan Central Railroad shops in Detroit recently a workman told him this story of a scene he had himself witnessed:

"Papa, will you please give me fifty cents for my spring hat? Most of the other girls have theirs already."

"No, not now, Jane, I can't spare the money."

A beautiful 10-year-old daughter had made the request. The disappointed girl went to school. The father started for his work. On his way to the shop he met a friend and being a hail fellow well met, he invited him into "Bill's" for a drink. There were others there and the father treated the crowd, and then threw down a dollar that just paid for the drinks.

Just then the saloonkeeper's daughter entered, and going behind the bar said: "Papa, I want one dollar for my spring hat."

"All right," said the dealer, as he pushed to her the dollar just laid on the bar.

Jane's father was dazed, walked out alone and said to himself. "I couldn't give my daughter fifty cents for her hat, but I had to bring my dollar here for the rum seller's daughter to buy a hat with. I'll never drink another drop."

YOUR DAUGHTER? THEN VOTE AGAINST THE SALOON.

This antisaloon poster argues, that when a man decides whether or not to drink, he is really deciding whether to provide for his own daughter or the saloonkeeper's daughter.

of the United Mine Workers at the time, said, "There is no easier way possible to make the unfortunate man or oppressed worker content with his misfortune than a couple of glasses of beer."[19]

Saloons were used as meeting places for larger groups, too. Political parties would hold their preliminary elections (called caucuses) there. Also, companies would go to a saloon to find workers. A town saloon would also operate as a small bank by cashing checks. In some cases, people could even get their mail at a saloon.

As more and more saloons opened across the country and catered to the immigrants, the middle class began to take a stronger position against alcohol.

TEMPERANCE GROUPS

A great number of the early pilgrims drank alcoholic beverages. Not all of them did, though. Even in the 1600s there were opponents of alcohol.

Many religious groups, including the Methodists and the Lutherans, were opposed to drinking. Their traditions were based on biblical teachings. Many sermons in colonial America preached against drunkenness. It was considered a sin by some. However, most ministers, educators, and civic leaders suggested that people drink in moderation, rather than give up drinking entirely.

In the mid-1600s, Peter Stuyvesant, the governor of New Amsterdam (which would later become New York), tried to control the spread of indecent taverns that were referred to as bawdyhouses. But the wealthy men who owned these taverns did not want anyone to cut their profits, so more and more taverns continued to open.

For a short time in the early 1700s, Plymouth officials tried issuing licenses as a way to regulate the increase in pubs, another name for saloons. But, since so many people liked to drink, regulations were usually ignored.

John Adams noted in his diary on February 29, 1760, that the taverns were "becoming the eternal haunt of loose, disorderly people."[1]

Dr. Benjamin Rush was a physician who served in the American Revolution and one of the men who signed the Declaration of Independence. He was among the first to question the popular idea that unlimited alcohol was actually good for the body and could cure illnesses. He tried to educate people about the medical, moral, and social costs of heavy drinking. In 1784, he published a pamphlet, called "Inquiry into the Effects of Spiritous Liquors on the Human Body and Mind." In this pamphlet he said that moderate amounts of wine and beer are not harmful. Drinking whiskey and rum, however, he felt led to disease and death. Whiskey and rum contain much larger quantities of alcohol than wine or beer. This may have been the reason he felt they were more dangerous. Rush advised people to stay away from distilled liquor. He was not in favor of legalized prohibition, but he did feel that drinking too much ruined lives and damaged society.

Temperance Groups Form

In the early 1800s, temperance groups began to form to try to convince people not to drink. Individuals and small groups of people began to pledge that they would not drink distilled liquor.

The word "temperance" means moderation. However, the temperance movement first advocated doing without any distilled liquor, rather than moderate use of it. Later, the movement pro-moted doing without any form of alcohol. Temperance groups worked closely with churches. Some religious groups (including Methodists and Lutherans) thought that alcohol was a primary cause of sin and that drinkers would not go to heaven.

The Massachusetts Society for the Suppression of Intemperance

One of the first temperance organizations in the country was the Massachusetts Society for the Suppression of Intemperance (MSSI). It was started in 1813. Its members had to be elected, and they paid dues of two dollars. The MSSI was not as bold as later temperance organizations. It did not hold public meetings or publish and distribute temperance literature. Instead, it promoted temperance through the social influence of its wealthy members. It encouraged employers to stop providing alcohol for their workers. The group urged local and state authorities to enforce tavern regulations and to carefully review license holders.

Between the 1730s and 1770s, a greater interest in religious beliefs and practices swept the American colonies. This was known as the First Great Awakening. The temperance movement was beginning to grow at the same time that the Second Great Awakening was taking place. The Second Great Awakening was a series of religious revivals that took place between 1795 and 1837. These revivals and the temperance movement seemed to go hand in hand. They supported many of the same beliefs or principles and encouraged much of the same behavior regarding alcohol.

In 1826, a Connecticut preacher named Lyman Beecher published his thoughts on the subject of temperance as "Six Sermons on the Nature, Occasions, Signs, Evils, and Remedy of Intemperance." Beecher said the only way to solve the evils of alcohol was to get everyone to stop drinking entirely. He was most concerned with the evils involved in the sale of liquor. Beecher felt that "Drunkards, no more than murderers, shall inherit the Kingdom of God." Beecher moved to Boston and worked there with others to try to unite small temperance groups around the country into a national temperance society.

One of the most popular preachers of the day who spoke out against intemperance was Reverend Justin Edwards. Edwards warned his listeners that liquor "has been among the more constant and fruitful sources of all our woes."[2]

Around this time, physicians began to spread an unusual myth, which they claimed was scientific fact. They said excessive drinking could lead to spontaneous combustion of the body. This meant the body would burst into flames for no apparent reason. These physicians believed that flammable alcohol fumes would seep out of a drinker's skin.

Nineteenth-century medical journals listed many cases of drunken people bursting into flames when coming too close to a candle. And, according to the journals, sometimes a person who drank would suddenly explode.

Dr. Eliphalet Nott, president of Union College in Schenectady, New York, was an expert on this kind of spontaneous combustion. Nott believed that these kinds of deaths had become so numerous that there was no need to question their existence.[3] Spontaneous

SOURCE DOCUMENT

A pledge I make, no wine to take;
Not brandy red, that turns the head;
Nor whisky hot, that makes the sot [drunk];
Nor fiery rum, that ruins the home.
Nor will I sin, by drinking gin;
Hard cider, too, will never do;
Nor lager beer, my heart to cheer;
Nor sparkling ale, my face to pale.
To quench [fulfill] *my thirst I'll always bring,*
Cold water from the well or spring;
So here I pledge perpetual hate,
To all that can intoxicate.[4]

This temperance pledge was printed in 1889 in Dr. Chase's Last Complete Work *by Ann Arbor doctor A.W. Chase.*

combustion from drinking alcohol is widely considered merely a myth today, however.

Throughout this period, there were all sorts of ideas concerning what to do about liquor. Some societies encouraged members to take a pledge that allowed them to drink light wines and beer. This was a "short pledge." Others took the "long pledge," promising they would not drink any form of alcohol. These members had the letter *T* for "total" put after their names. They were called teetotalers. Later, "teetotaler" came to mean anyone who would not drink any alcohol, not just those who took the pledge.

During and after the Second Great Awakening, there was a general movement to improve both physical and moral aspects of humanity. There were separate groups designed to better mankind in different ways. There were temperance movements, peace movements, and religious revivals. Even stopping the Sunday mail was an issue that involved reformists. The abolition of slavery became the biggest reform movement before the Civil War. Many of these reform movements had separate organizations, but many people joined more than one movement.

The Washingtonians

In the 1840s, a new temperance group formed when several friends who were heavy drinkers decided to stop drinking for good. They wanted to reform other drinkers, too. They called themselves Washingtonians, after George Washington, their hero of the American

Revolution. At their meetings, drinkers told how they had given up alcohol. Then they signed a pledge to give up all drinking. The meetings attracted many people. These meetings received much attention, especially in many small cities and towns. Hundreds of Washingtonian societies were formed. They were located in scattered towns and rural communities. Without continued support, much of the interest died out as soon as the meetings were over. Due to the loss of interest, many of these groups ceased to exist. Within a short time, the entire Washingtonian movement ended.

The First State Liquor Law

In 1851, Maine was the first state to pass a law forbidding the manufacture and sale of any intoxicating liquor within the state. Prohibitionists, sometimes called drys, were happy. Lyman Beecher said, "That glorious Maine Law was a square and grand blow right between the horns of the Devil."[5] Maine's new liquor law contained provisions for fines, prison for repeat offenders, searches, seizures, and even raids on liquor stocks. It was almost as complicated as the Volstead Act would be in 1920.

In the next four years, Ohio, Illinois, Rhode Island, Vermont, Michigan, Indiana, Iowa, Minnesota, Massachusetts, Connecticut, Pennsylvania, and New York adopted their own liquor laws. Delaware passed its first Prohibition law right after Maine, but the law was declared unconstitutional the next year.

The Civil War

During the 1850s and on through the Civil War (1861–1865), most Americans were more concerned about whether or not to end slavery than they were about alcohol. However, once again, the government found a use for alcohol. On July 1, 1862, President Abraham Lincoln signed the Internal Revenue Act. This act was created to raise money for the war. Under this act, saloon and tavern owners had to pay a fee. The act also placed a tax by the gallon on the manufacture of liquor and beer. Many people did not like this, however. They felt this act meant the government was approving the liquor business.

The National Prohibition Party

After the Civil War, when the issue of slavery was resolved, the use of alcohol became one of the most important issues in America. Many former abolitionists turned to the temperance movement as a new cause.

A number of temperance leaders decided the time had come to form a political party dedicated to the fight against alcohol. The National Prohibition party was founded in 1869. Its main purpose was to work for Prohibition. It was also in favor of giving women the right to vote and the direct election of senators. (Up until the ratification of the Seventeenth Amendment in 1913, a state's senators were elected by its legislature, not the people.) These reforms would all eventually become part of the Constitution through amendments.

In 1872, the first National Prohibition party candidate for the presidency was James Black. He was a lawyer from Pennsylvania. Black did not receive a large number of votes. Future candidates did not, either. The Prohibition party, however, did help the American people accept the idea that the Constitution should be amended to outlaw alcohol.

The Women's Crusade

Alcohol had always been the greatest contributing cause of social and domestic problems in America. Families had been the ones to feel the negative effects of alcohol since husbands were typically the family members who drank. When the breadwinner of the family was an alcoholic and could not hold a job, it was not easy for the wife to find employment that would allow her to support the family. Therefore, it was only natural that women should be the ones to want to put an end to alcohol use.

In 1873, a doctor named Dio Lewis spoke out against alcohol in many towns in New York, Pennsylvania, and Ohio. Lewis told listeners that he believed women could close the saloons of America if they took to the streets to do it. On December 23, 1873, he spoke in a little town called Hillsboro, Ohio. More than sixty women stood up at the end of his lecture. They were ready to accept his challenge to close the saloons. The next day, a sixty-year-old housewife named Eliza Thompson, the town's most prominent woman, was chosen to be their leader. Thompson read

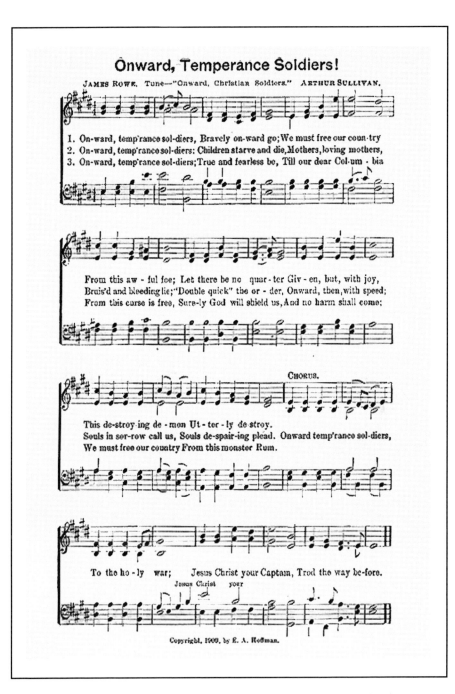

Songs such as this one were used to motivate those involved in the temperance movement. The lyrics of this song show that many temperance workers were also very religious.

from the Bible and said a prayer. Next, singing a hymn, she led the women of Hillsboro out of the church where they had gathered.

The women marched down the town's main street, to the drugstores where liquor was sold. Next, they went to the saloons. They stood or kneeled in front of each saloon, singing hymns and praying. Sometimes they went inside to demand that the sale of liquor be stopped.

In town after town, women took to the streets. They marched from saloon to saloon. The movement quickly became known as the Women's Crusade.

Often, the women were called names, or they were pushed as they approached a saloon. Their clothes were ripped, and their hair was pulled. In some cases, they were pelted with rotten eggs or soaked with water or beer.

However, between January and July 1874, thousands of saloons were closed by the Women's Crusade. One such closing occurred in Xenia, Ohio. A reporter who witnessed the event explained what he saw when he ran across the street from the hotel where he was staying. "The Shades of Death [a saloon] has surrendered . . . Mr. Steve Phillips, of the "Shades of Death," invited the ladies to enter, and announced that he gave up everything to them, and would never sell anything intoxicating in Xenia again."[6]

The Women's Christian Temperance Union

In 1874, Presbyterian Church organizers in Cleveland, Ohio, who had followed the crusade called a meeting.

This meeting led to the establishment of the Women's Christian Temperance Union (WCTU), with Annie Wittenmyer as its first president. This organization was even more effective than the Women's Crusade.

In 1876, Frances Elizabeth Willard, a former university professor, became the WCTU's second president. Willard was an ex-crusader and a born leader. It was not long before she had chapters of the WCTU in every state. Willard was also an early feminist, wanting equal rights for women. She believed that "Drink and tobacco are the great separatists [sic] between men and women. Once they used these things together, but woman's evolution has carried her beyond them."[7] By this, Willard meant that taverns or saloons were separating men and women because they were places for men only. Yet, Willard felt they were bad places, where men should not want to go either.

Willard was one of the first activists to promote nationwide Prohibition. Later, the WCTU would help make Prohibition a reality.

In 1881, Kansas was the first state to make Prohibition part of its state constitution. Several other states followed with constitutional Prohibition. Even more states continued to work on Prohibition laws.

The most radical and vocal member of the WCTU was a woman from Kansas named Carry Nation. Nation did not like it that no one obeyed her state's law against alcohol, and that saloons operated openly. In 1899, Nation charged into Mort Strong's saloon in Medicine Lodge, Kansas, with a hatchet. She smashed

The American Bond--Loyalty

QUESTION BOX No. 1

1. What is the American Bond?

The bond of loyalty, which firmly binds all patriots in our United States of America.

2. What is the American Bond Emblem?

The American Flag---

> "With its red for love, and its white for law
> And its blue for the hope that our fathers saw
> Of a larger liberty,"

as Frances Willard said.

3. What is the Badge of the American Bond?

Our National Shield with the words, "American Bond--- Loyalty" and "In God We Trust." With lifted hands together we pledge loyalty to flag and law.

4. What is the Creed of the American Bond?

THE AMERICAN'S CREED

I BELIEVE in the United States of America as a government of the people, by the people, for the people; whose just powers are derived from the consent of the governed; a democracy in a republic; a sovereign nation of many sovereign states; a perfect union, one and inseparable, established upon those principles of freedom, equality, justice and humanity for which American patriots sacrificed their lives and fortunes.

I therefore believe it is my duty to my country to love it, to support its constitution; to obey its laws; to respect its flag; and to defend it against all enemies.

5. What is the Pledge of the American Bond?

I pledge allegiance to my flag, and to the republic for which it stands, one nation, indivisible, with liberty and justice for all.

6. And now a rousing yell for the American Bond!

> Hear Ye! Hear Ye!
> Who are We? Who are We?
> Patriots of the American Bond!
> We shout for the flag and a nation free!
> "Obedience to law is LIBERTY!"
> Hear YE! Hear YE!
> HEAR YE-E-E!!!

Song: *"The Star Spangled Banner"*

This pledge card for the American Bond quotes Francis Willard's comments about the American flag. Willard's desire for a better America fueled her involvement in the WCTU.

everything she could. She continued a series of raids like this all over Kansas. She smashed plate-glass windows, defaced paintings, and destroyed kegs of rum and whiskey in almost every saloon she raided. Soon she showed up in other states all across America, wrecking saloons. She became a big star with the media. Songs were written about her. She sold miniature hatchets and autographed postcards of herself by mail. All this helped the temperance movement by giving it much attention.

Eventually, the WCTU did not want to be associated with Nation. Her behavior was too outrageous. People either laughed at her or were afraid of her. Nation's money ran out, and the media lost interest.

The Anti-Saloon League

Another American temperance organization, the Ohio Anti-Saloon League, was formed on May 24, 1893, in Oberlin, Ohio. Reverend Howard Hyde Russell was elected its first state superintendent. The league focused on the saloon, not just alcohol. The league printed many publications that called for an end to saloons that were "annually sending thousands of our youths to destruction, for corrupting politics, dissipating workmen's wages, leading astray 60,000 girls each year into lives of immorality and banishing children from school."[8] One league member explained that the saloon must be destroyed because:

> It contributes so largely to human sorrow. The men who are fighting through the Anti-Saloon League are

RAILROADS NEED SOBER EMPLOYES

WHY?

"Two Fingers of Red Liquor can Turn a Ten-Million-Dollar Safety Block Signal In to a Ten-Million Dollar Waste of Money."

Many people felt that alcohol was a major cause for accidents in the workplace.

not 'professional reformers' nor are they men looking for political preferment. They are businessmen, patriotic citizens who recognize the danger in the continuance of the saloon and have set themselves the task to wipe it out of existence.[9]

During the 1890s, the league led the temperance movement. It was very successful in raising funds, mainly through church organizations. The league appealed to church members in small towns all across the country to make their local, state, and national representatives respond to the temperance movement.

Ernest H. Cherrington, who later wrote about the history of the league, said, "the movement was dependent upon the church, first of all, for financial support. It was also dependent upon the church for the necessary influence and power to turn the tide. . . ."[10]

This political cartoon depicts liquor as an octopus trying to strangle the world. Each of the octopus's tentacles represents a different negative effect liquor has on people. The club of "American anti-saloon methods" seems the only way for the world to rid itself of the liquor octopus.

The Anti-Saloon League was established on a national basis in 1896. Russell was named the first superintendent of the national league.

The Anti-Saloon League used the political system to support its cause, but it did not support only members of the Prohibition party. Instead, the league supported politicians from any party who voted for Prohibition. The Anti-Saloon League produced all sorts of pamphlets and newspapers filled with information against liquor. Its motto was, The saloon must go.

By the turn of the century, the Anti-Saloon League had growing control over many state lawmakers. It was working to gain more power at the national level.

Prohibition and Women's Suffrage

By 1915, it was becoming clearer and clearer that Prohibition and women's suffrage were two closely related issues. The Flying Squadron of America was a temperance group that wanted to educate Americans about the evils of alcohol. The squadron consisted of three groups of traveling lecturers who visited cities from September 30, 1914, to June 6, 1915, delivering speeches.

In a 1915 lecture, Dr. Carolyn E. Geisel, a member of the squadron, made it clear how the two issues were related:

> You have driven us to take a firm stand these days. There is not a right-minded woman in the United States of America who would ever have dreamed of asking for the ballot if you men had done your duty by

Dr. Carolyn E. Geisel

A perfect dynamo of power.—*Paul M. Pearson.*
The biggest little woman in the world.—*Dr. W. L. Davidson.*
A womanly woman, a powerful speaker, a crystal clear soul.—*Former Governor Johnson, of Minnesota.*

Dr. Carolyn E. Geisel was able to clearly explain the connection between the need for Prohibition and the need for women's suffrage (the right to vote).

your own home. But you did not do it . . . We are asking for the ballot that we may defend our own business, and when we get the ballot you may just as well know what we will do with it. We will be true to our housekeeping instincts. We will just roll that ballot into a mop and wipe up the last inch of wet territory around about us.[11]

By "wet," Geisel meant territory where alcohol was still allowed.

World War I

On April 6, 1917, the United States declared war on Germany and entered World War I. Prohibitionists worked to shut down the liquor industry. Congress passed a number of wartime Prohibition measures. These included a food control bill designed to conserve grain and other food for the war effort. This bill banned the use of foodstuffs (like grain) in the making of

This antialcohol poster appealed to patriotic Americans during World War I.

When Sammie Comes Marching Home—What Then?

IS IT NOT ENOUGH
THAT THEY
DIE FOR THE FLAG?
--
WHY SHOULD
WE COMPEL THEM
TO DIE
FROM
DRINK?
--
VOTE DRY

SERIES A. No. 1

24x36 inches, on heavy paper, tinted
Printed attractively in buff and brown
See prices on tinted separate sheet

distilled liquor. Basically, this ban shut down the distilleries. Beer and wine were still produced. However, Congress gave President Wilson the power to order that beer contain less alcohol, and he did. Congress also ordered liquor-free zones around military bases.

The Anti-Saloon League used the outbreak of the war to its advantage. It declared that Prohibition would help win the war. Therefore, it was the only patriotic choice. The league pointed out that many brewers were German Americans. It accused the brewing industry of being pro-German.

Prohibitionists warned, "Pro-Germanism is only the froth from the German beer saloon. Our German Socialist party and the German-American Alliance are the spawn of the beer-saloon."[12]

In the Senate, anti-Prohibitionists, sometimes called wets, let it be known that they would not object to a vote now on the proposal for the Eighteenth Amendment. However, there was one condition. They insisted that, once the proposal passed in the Senate and the House, it would have to be ratified in six (later modified to seven) years. Prohibitionists agreed to this condition. This greatly pleased the anti-Prohibitionists, who felt sure that six years would not be enough time for ratification. If they could delay ratification in just thirteen states, they could defeat the amendment.

However, the amendment did pass, and a new decade was just around the corner. Americans knew they were in for changes now. But they did not realize just how many changes they would be facing as the 1920s roared in.

THE ROARING TWENTIES

Before 1920, most Americans worked long, hard days for low to moderate pay, yet enjoyed few conveniences that people today take for granted.

As the 1920s began, women dressed conservatively in ankle-length dresses and sensible shoes. Most women pulled their hair back into a neat bun. Women did not have the right to vote. If they worked outside the home, they often made much less money than men did for the same job. Travel was more difficult. Trips had to be taken by train.

All this would change during the 1920s, largely because of many amazing technological, social, and political advances that occurred then. The 1920s were not a quiet, passive time. They "roared" with activity as much of the population moved from small towns and farms to the faster-paced cities. Because of this increased activity, the decade was called the Roaring Twenties. F. Scott Fitzgerald, author of the famous 1920s novel *The Great Gatsby*, described this period as "the greatest, gaudiest spree in history."[1]

One of the biggest political advances of the century took place on August 26, 1920. The Nineteenth

Antialcohol ads continued to be published, even after the Eighteenth Amendment was passed.

Amendment was passed. It gave women the right to vote. Now, women had a say in what happened in their country and in their neighborhoods. They finally had some real power.

Flappers

Women felt freer now, too. Before the 1920s, it was hard to imagine women smoking or drinking in public. However, they soon began to engage in these activities more often. Also during this new era, young women cut their hair. Short haircuts called bobs were the rage all across the country.

As the 1920s moved along, women wore shorter dresses and long, beaded necklaces. They rolled their stockings down below their knees as they did wild dances like the Charleston and the tango. These free-spirited young women were nicknamed flappers in 1915 by journalist and social critic H. L. Mencken.[2]

Two flappers do a popular dance on a wall in Washington, D.C.

Fads and Crazes

Wages increased for many workers during the 1920s, while the workweek became shorter. This meant that some Americans had more money to spend and more free time to spend it. An average American's disposable income (the money not required for bills and other expenses) went up. For the top one percent of wealthiest Americans, the money they had available to spend went up by 75 percent more than that of other people. This made the gap between the economic classes even wider.

Many Americans were willing to take chances to find fun wherever and whenever they could. As a result, all sorts of silly fads and crazes developed. Couples danced for days at exhausting dance marathons. People swallowed whole goldfish or sat on flagpoles for hours and hours (to see who could stay there the longest). One person who sat on flagpoles all across the United States was Alvin "Shipwreck" Kelly. Kelly would sit on a pole for weeks, in the rain and sun, trying to beat his previous record; then he would move on to another location to attempt a new record.[3]

Sports

America was wild about sports in the 1920s. Babe Ruth became the first baseball player to be traded for $125,000. Professional football was founded in September 1920. College football was big, too. Notre Dame coach Knute Rockne and his group of players nicknamed the Four Horsemen became quite famous.

Jack Dempsey was world heavyweight boxing champion from 1919 to 1926.

People enjoyed watching professional golf or the amateur games of Bobby Jones. Bill Tilden and Helen Wills Moody were amateur tennis stars of the times.

The Olympics were popular, too. Paavo Nurmi, one of the "Flying Finns" of Norway, was a famous runner. Johnny Weismuller was a great swimmer. He later starred in a series of *Tarzan* movies.

Gertrude Ederle became the first woman to swim across the English Channel. She beat the previous best time by almost two hours.

Jack Dempsey became boxing heavyweight champion of the world in 1919. Boxing became a big business.

Other fantastic accomplishments gained public attention at this time, also. Charles Lindbergh's 1927 transatlantic solo plane flight captured the era's feeling of excitement and daring exploits. People were in awe of "Lucky Lindy" or "the Lone Eagle" for his achievement. An extravagant New York ticker-tape parade was given in Lindbergh's honor when he completed his famous flight.

The Movies

Movies were a favorite form of entertainment during Prohibition, just as they are today. Hollywood became the movie capital of the world in the 1920s. Audiences saw things in movies they had never seen before—sex, gambling, and drinking.

Clara Bow was a famous movie star of the times. Every girl wanted to look like her. Bow was nicknamed the "It Girl" because she had "it," which was sex appeal, and everyone wanted "it."[4]

New Foods

Many foods that people still enjoy today were created in the 1920s. A soft drink called Howdy emerged in 1920, but in a few years the name was changed to 7-Up.

Several candy bars were introduced in the 1920s, including Baby Ruth, Mounds, Milky Way, and Reese's Peanut Butter Cup.

In 1927, a chemist in Hastings, Nebraska, invented an unusual beverage called Kool-Aid. People could make their own refreshing drink at home by mixing this flavored powder with a pitcher of water and a cup of sugar.

Kraft's Velveeta became available in 1928, and Rice Krispies cereal hit the market that same year.

The Automobile

Before the 1920s, very few people had their own automobile. Americans were used to paying for everything except their mortgage in cash, and automobiles were just too expensive. There were no credit cards like MasterCard or Visa, and no easy payment plans for products many Americans wanted. If they could not afford to pay cash for a product, people simply did not buy it.

Henry Ford, maker of the Model T, wanted everyone to have one of his automobiles. By the mid-1920s, he had dropped the price of a Model T from $950 to $290. Thanks to the assembly line, a car could be produced in about ninety minutes, compared to the fourteen hours it had taken before. As a result, cars were not only more affordable, there were more of them available. Everyone wanted an automobile, and now Americans could buy one on credit and make

Calvin Coolidge was the president during most of the Roaring Twenties, from 1923 to 1929.

payments until the loan was paid off. Soon, more and more families had an automobile. By 1929, over 23 million Americans owned their own car. The automobile gave Americans more freedom to come and go as they pleased.

The Radio

When Americans were not at the theater watching the latest movie, they were often at home, listening to the radio. The golden years of radio would not arrive until the 1930s, but live sporting events, such as the World Series and heavyweight fights, were first broadcast in the 1920s.

Advertising was a big part of radio. It began to change now, too. Manufacturers wanted everyone to buy their products. The best way to get people to do this was to convince them their lives would be better if they did. Advertisers started campaigns to convince people they would be happier, more successful, and more popular if they bought the right toothpaste, wore the right clothes, and owned all the latest gadgets and modern-day conveniences. This new advertising sold what advertisers still call "the sizzle instead of the steak," and it worked. The older generation had been cautious and conservative. Now the younger generation wanted to try everything.

The Volstead Act was designed to prevent people from drinking any beverage with more than one half of one percent of alcohol. This seemed unreasonable to many people, and they ignored the law. They knew it was not an easy law to enforce. There were just too many exceptions to the rule.

ILLEGAL LIQUOR

Homemade Liquor

People could make cider at home, then store it so it "hardened." This meant it became alcoholic. Hard cider was not illegal as long as no alcohol was actually added to the cider and the maker did not try to sell it.

Beer could still be legally brewed, too. (Even Sears sold equipment for brewing beer.) Before it was sold, however, most of the alcohol had to be removed. This was called "near beer." People did not care for it very much, so it was often sprayed with alcohol from a hypodermic needle to make it more like "real" beer. It was illegal to do this, but "needle beer" became very popular during Prohibition.

The California grape growers could no longer make wine. Still, they provided consumers with another way

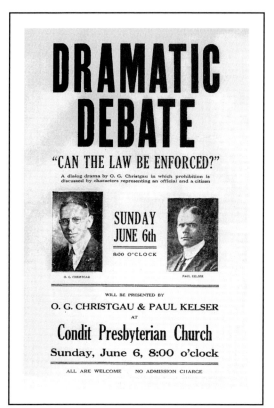

DRAMATIC DEBATE

"CAN THE LAW BE ENFORCED?"

A dialog drama by O. G. Christgau in which prohibition is discussed by characters representing an official and a citizen

SUNDAY JUNE 6th

8:00 O'CLOCK

O. G. CHRISTGAU   PAUL KELSER

WILL BE PRESENTED BY

O. G. CHRISTGAU & PAUL KELSER

AT

Condit Presbyterian Church

Sunday, June 6, 8:00 o'clock

ALL ARE WELCOME   NO ADMISSION CHARGE

From Prohibition's very beginning, people debated whether the Volstead Act could be enforced.

around the law against alcohol. Fruit Industries, Inc., was a company made up of most of the California grape growers. It produced a product called Vine-Glo, which was used to make grape juice. The literature that came with the Vine-Glo instructed buyers what *not* to do. If customers did the things the literature told them not to, the grape juice would turn into wine in sixty days. So, really, they were telling customers how to make wine. Americans bought a lot of Vine-Glo, and the demand grew. Grape growers had 97,000 acres devoted to grapes for "juice" in 1919, but by 1926, they had devoted 681,000 acres for Vine-Glo "juice." In 1929, the U.S. government loaned the grape growers money for more land.[1]

LESS DRINK MORE HOMES

Henry living in a wet State, found it easy to spend a dollar a week for beer. After 25 years all there was to show for his money was a pile of empty beer kegs—and he did not own those.

John, living in a dry State, found it easy to put a dollar a week into the Building Loan Association. After 25 years he owned a *good home.*

Sobriety Fosters the Clear Brain, the Steady Hand, the Thrift Habit

No. 75

This poster suggests that a person who does not drink is more likely to be able to afford a home for his or her family.

There were other fairly easy ways to obtain alcohol. Although it was illegal to distill alcohol at home, the equipment to do this cost only a few dollars and the instructions for distilling were easy to get. The government had published bulletins between 1906 and 1910 that explained how to distill alcohol from sugar beets, grain, and potato peelings. Bathtub gin became very popular during Prohibition, too. It was called this because so much water was required to make it that the only place big enough to hold the container for it was a bathtub.

Misusing Legal Liquor

Under the Volstead Act, liquor could still be bought legally for medicinal purposes. As a result, many prescriptions were written by dishonest doctors. With these prescriptions, liquor could then be obtained at government warehouses and mixed with other liquids to make even bigger supplies of alcoholic drinks. Dishonest druggists filled thousands of these prescriptions, too.

It was also still possible for churches to purchase sacramental wine, used for religious purposes. It was very difficult to monitor this part of the liquor business. The demand for sacramental wines increased by eight hundred thousand gallons during the first two years of Prohibition. The spokesman for the Federal Council of the Churches of Christ in America said, "not more than one-quarter of this is sacramental—the rest is sacrilegious [against religion]."[2]

Enforcing the Volstead Act

Still, in the early 1920s, Wayne Wheeler and many other advocates of Prohibition felt that the Volstead Act could easily be enforced, and it would not cost the country much money to do so. They thought that once Americans saw the positive effects of a "dry" nation (meaning a nation without alcohol), the need for law enforcement would disappear.

There were others who were serious about enforcing the Volstead Act, too. In September 1922, Henry Ford had a notice posted on the walls of his automobile factory in Detroit. Although Ford fired people for many reasons, this notice let workers know that it would cost a man his job "to have the odor of beer, wine or liquor on his breath, or to have any of these intoxicants on his person or in his home."[3] Ford said he would

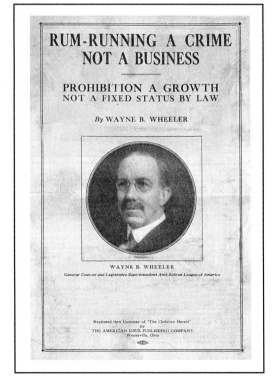

Wayne Wheeler, who had authored the Volstead Act, felt that Prohibition could be easily enforced.

enforce the law to the letter. He was so serious about this that he used a private police force to spy on his workers. Any worker caught buying or drinking hard liquor was fired.

The U.S. government seemed serious about enforcing the Volstead Act, too. The first year of Prohibition, Congress set aside $6.35 million to enforce the Volstead Act. Each year, more and more money was needed.

Agents of the Prohibition Unit of the U.S. Department of Justice—called the Prohibition Bureau—had their work cut out for them. There were about fifteen hundred of these agents. They were poorly paid and poorly trained. Many were corrupt. People hated them everywhere they went.

Two of the most successful Prohibition agents were friends Isidor Einstein and Moe Smith. They were a colorful pair and were known as Izzy and Moe by Americans who read about them in the newspapers. Izzy and Moe worked as Prohibition Bureau agents for five years. During that time, they were able to arrest almost five thousand suspects. They often wore clever disguises so they would be allowed to enter places where liquor was sold. They impersonated everyone from tourists to gravediggers. They also liked to invite the press along when they were about to make an arrest because they loved the publicity. Their pictures were in the newspapers all the time. People laughed at their crazy costumes and unusual methods. Eventually, they became too successful. The officials they worked for were jealous and felt this dynamic duo was making a mockery of justice, so Izzy and Moe were fired.[4]

Bad Liquor

A large amount of alcohol that was sold during Prohibition was just plain dangerous. Industrial alcohol was used in many products such as toothpaste or paint. This alcohol was poisonous. The poisons could be removed, but it still would not taste very good. It is not surprising then that mixed drinks, known as cocktails, became popular during Prohibition. Other ingredients could cover up the bad taste of the industrial alcohol. In many cases, the poisons were not removed from industrial alcohol before it was sold for consumption.

Liquor packed in metals such as tin was dangerous, too. The chemical interaction of the alcohol with the metal produced deadly toxins. During Prohibition, the death rate from poisonous alcohol was very high. It soared from 1,064 in 1920 to 4,154 in 1925.[5] According to Edward Behr, author of *Prohibition: Thirteen Years that Changed America*, by 1927, deaths caused by poisonous alcohol may have been more than fifty thousand.[6] There were also hundreds of thousands of cases of blindness and paralysis caused by poisonous alcohol.

Speakeasies Replace Saloons

While Prohibition did not keep people from drinking alcohol, it did change where and how they drank it.

Now, drinking had to be done in secret, out-of-the-way places. Saloons shut down. They were replaced by speakeasies. Since alcohol was no longer available for legal purchase, even the middle class went to speakeasies. With both the middle and lower classes as customers, speakeasies were more respectable than saloons, which had only attracted the lower class.

Speakeasies were secret clubs with false fronts that made them look like ordinary grocery stores or warehouses from the outside. Inside, there were sliding doors or hidden panels that led to rooms where alcohol was served. It was often necessary to know a code phrase, such as "Joe sent me," to be allowed inside the speakeasy.

Some "speaks" ran legitimate restaurants. The drinking was done from the back room where customers might be asked to "speak easy" so they could not be heard from the restaurant. By 1922, there were an estimated 32,000 to 100,000 speakeasies in New York City alone.

Grover A. Whalen, police commissioner of New York City said, "All you need is two bottles and a room and you have a speakeasy."[7] He may have exaggerated, but many speakeasies were small and dirty. Others were large and fancy and featured entertainment as well as alcohol. Musician Duke Ellington and singer Cab Calloway started their careers in speakeasies. The most impressive speakeasies had large bars with many bartenders and featured elaborate shows.

DAN BEARD AND BOYS

Dan Beard, one of the founders of the Boy Scouts of America, believed that Prohibition helped contribute to the improvement of both the mind and body.

Many of these big, high-priced speakeasies were owned or controlled by gangsters, yet it was two women who competed for the crown of queen of the speakeasies. Both operated in New York City. Belle Livingston ran a five-story club on East Fifty-eighth Street. It was called the Country Club. A code phrase would not get anyone inside the Country Club, but five dollars would. Once inside, the upper floors were available only for guests who ordered many drinks throughout the evening. Here, they could play table tennis or miniature golf and order champagne for forty dollars a bottle.

Mary Louise "Texas" Guinan ran the El Fay Club at 107 West Forty-fifth Street. This club was backed by gangster Larry Fay. Guinan would greet guys with the words "Hello, sucker." This became a catchphrase of the Prohibition era.

Most speakeasies were not very grand, but the rich and poor alike could be found there, looking for alcohol.

Hiding Liquor

During Prohibition, some people carried alcohol around with them in a hip flask. This was a slim container that was hidden at the hip or in a large pocket. Women could hide a bottle of liquor in their garter belts. Hollowed-out books, lunch buckets, and even backpacks were sometimes used to carry alcohol.

Bootleggers, Smugglers, and Gangsters

All this alcohol had to come from somewhere. Since it could not be purchased legally, and not everyone who drank made their own, many turned to the bootlegger.

Bootleggers were people who sold illegal liquor. The name "bootlegger" probably came about in the early 1880s when the sale of alcohol was prohibited in Kansas and Oklahoma. At that time, people operated illegal stills and came to town to sell their illegal liquor, called moonshine. They hid the bottles of illegal liquor in their boots. In the 1920s, anyone who sold illegal liquor was called a bootlegger.

Most people did not think of the neighborhood bootlegger as a criminal, though. He was just someone providing a popular product.

Much of the illegal liquor at the time came from Canada, Mexico, and the Caribbean. Smugglers called rumrunners used small boats that had secret compartments and false bottoms. Although these rumrunners sold their illegal liquor for three to four times what they had paid for it, many times the liquor they sold was diluted with water to make larger amounts. One smuggler named William (Big Bill) McCoy transported his cargo aboard a schooner named the *Tomoka*. McCoy liked to brag that he smuggled only the best, undiluted whiskey, which he called "the real McCoy."

Illegal liquor soon became one of the biggest businesses in the country. Organized crime grew like never before. Smugglers had to be willing to battle it out with the police, the Coast Guard, or anyone else who tried to take their stash. Violence was just part of the business. Big-time gangsters knew they could make big-time money smuggling and selling alcohol.

6

THE GROWTH OF ORGANIZED CRIME

There were a lot of ways to make money from illegal liquor once Prohibition started. Producing and selling alcohol were very profitable, but so was smuggling it. One group of criminals would produce and sell the alcohol. Another group would secretly transport it. These gangs or "organizations" in one city formed ties with organizations in other cities. This was because so many varieties of liquor were in demand, and a single producer could not manufacture or distribute every variety. Many organizations specialized in a few varieties of liquor. Large organizations had connections to other organizations.

Alcohol was a profitable but dangerous business. While bootleggers would smuggle the alcohol, other criminals would try to hijack the bootleggers' supplies. Often, liquor was hijacked from ships or trucks that were used to transport it, or it was taken from warehouses where it was stored. Bootleggers kept the locations of their warehouses secret to prevent this. They also hired gunmen to keep hijackers from taking liquor as it was being transported.

Gangs had their own distinct markets and territories, but there were big fights between competitive gangs. Each tried to take over the other's territory. In Chicago, gang battles resulted in the deaths of nearly eight hundred gangsters between 1920 to 1933.[1]

Gangs used machine guns and bombs to get rid of their enemies. Machine guns were lightweight. They could fire up to a thousand 45-caliber pistol cartridges a minute. Bombs were an even easier way to wipe out a rival because the bomber did not have to make a fast getaway after the killing. The bomber could plant the bomb and be miles away when it exploded.

Sometimes police officers and government agents were also dangerous. Many of the agents had never used firearms before, and they were poorly trained. They were sent out to fight gangsters who had submachine guns, pistols, shotguns, bombs, and other kinds of weapons. It was easy for innocent civilians to get caught in the cross fire.

Gangsters and regular citizens were not the only ones operating illegal speakeasies or smuggling alcohol. The government sometimes set up these kinds of illegal operations to entrap gangsters. The Bridge Whist Club in New York was one of the fanciest speakeasies of the times. Since it was run by the government, the taxpayers were footing the bill.[2]

A Glamorous Image

Gangster films were the action movies of the 1920s. They were very popular. A typical gangster film was full of car chases, double crosses, gunfire, and killings, with a love story usually thrown in. Of course, the movies glamorized gangsters. As a result, moviegoers were fascinated with gangsters' fancy cars, fancy clothes, and good-looking girlfriends. Gangster slang became popular, too. No one wanted to be known as a "stool pigeon" (an informer or spy), for example, but everyone wanted to be a "big shot" (an important person).

Officials on the Take

Bootleggers, speakeasy operators, and gangsters were not the only ones who wanted to make money from illegal alcohol. All across the country corrupt police officers and government officials made money in payoffs or bribes by ignoring the illegal activity taking place around them.

Even the agents of the Prohibition Bureau, who were supposed to enforce the new law, were mostly corrupt. They earned very little money as agents, but they could make a great deal when they helped smugglers or accepted bribes.

Members of the U.S. Coast Guard could also make big profits if they allowed rumrunners to bring as much liquor as they could into ports on the Atlantic, the Pacific, the Great Lakes, or the Gulf Coast. For many, this easy money was too good to pass up.

Al Capone

The biggest gangs back then were in Chicago and New York City, and the most legendary mobster of the

1920s was Al Capone. Capone had many nicknames, including Al, Big Al, and Snorky, but his most common nickname was Scarface. When he was a young man, Capone had been attacked by Frank Galluccio. Galluccio slashed Capone with a razor, and it left three horrible facial scars.

Capone was born in Brooklyn, New York, in 1899. He moved to Chicago in 1920 at the request of his longtime friend, gangster Johnny Torrio. Torrio worked for his uncle, Jim Colosimo, a big-time crime boss in Chicago. Colosimo was not interested in making huge profits from alcohol, and right

Al Capone was one of the most ruthless criminals who profited from illegal liquor sales during the Prohibition era.

after Prohibition started, Colosimo was killed. Torrio and Capone were suspected of killing Colosimo, but police had no proof that they were the ones who had shot Colosimo to death. With Colosimo gone, Torrio took over as gang leader. Capone was his right-hand man. Torrio retired in 1925 after he was almost killed by a rival gang. Capone took his place as the big boss.

Capone was a ruthless man. He once used a baseball bat to beat to death some rival mobsters he had invited to the Burnham Hotel for dinner. He wanted to show everyone that nobody should mess with him.

The St. Valentine's Day Massacre

Bugs Moran was boss of the North Side gang in Chicago. He was one of Capone's main rivals. Moran liked to have his gunmen and their cover men drive by in half a dozen cars and mow down their victims with machine guns.

Capone wanted Moran and most of his North Side gang eliminated. Capone, or one of his gang members, devised a plan.

Capone had a loyal bootlegger contact Moran and offer him a shipment of smuggled whiskey for a cheap price. The whiskey would be delivered to Moran's North Clark Street warehouse on February 14, Valentine's Day, 1929, at 10:30 in the morning. Moran told five of his men to meet him at the warehouse that day.

Valentine's Day morning in Chicago was snowy and cold. Moran's men waited for Moran at the warehouse.

Two other men joined Moran's gang there. One was Reinhardt Schwimmer, a young eye doctor who liked to hang out with gangsters. The other was Jon May, an auto mechanic Moran had hired.

Moran and two other members of his gang were running late. As Moran's car turned the corner onto North Clark Street, Moran spotted a police car driving up to the warehouse. Two men dressed as policemen and two other men dressed as civilians got out of the car. A fifth uniformed man stayed at the wheel. Moran figured it was just another typical police raid, and he did not feel like getting involved. He and his two men quickly left the scene before the police officers spotted them. This was lucky for Moran and his men, because these five imposters were actually Capone's hired killers.

Inside the warehouse, the seven men must have assumed the same thing Moran did—that this was a routine bust—because they followed directions and lined up against the wall. Capone's men then opened fire with Thompson submachine guns. They killed six of the seven men instantly.

Next, the uniformed men marched the plainclothes men out the front door with their hands raised, to make it look like an arrest was being made for the killings. Anyone watching this would think the policemen were carrying off some prisoners, as they all got into the police car and drove away.

When the real police arrived, the seventh man, Frank Gusenberg, was still alive, even though he had twenty-two bullet wounds. Police tried to get him to tell them who had done the shooting.

"No one, nobody shot me," was all Gusenberg would say.[3] He died a little while later.

It had been a brilliant plan, except for one thing. Bugs Moran was still alive.

Newspapers quickly called it the "St. Valentine's Day Massacre." Moran knew that Capone wanted him dead. Moran told authorities, "only Capone kills like that." But the police had no proof, and no one was ever tried for the killings.[4] Capone had wisely been in Miami at the time of the shootings.

The Untouchables

Enforcing Prohibition became more and more difficult. There were too many people who ignored the law. Many civic leaders, politicians, and police officers were not very interested in enforcing the Prohibition laws. A policeman's pay was low. Many times public leaders and policemen would take money to ignore the speakeasies and illegal alcohol sales. In Chicago, gangsters like Al Capone had a lot of money from the illegal liquor trade to use as bribes. Not all policemen were taking money, however.

In 1929, a former credit investigator named Elliott Ness joined the Department of Justice in Chicago. Ness suggested that a special unit be created that would report only to the highest officials. Six businessmen from the Chicago Association of Commerce persuaded the Department of Justice to follow this plan.

Nine agents were selected. Each one had a different skill that would help this secret squad. Some would wiretap the phones of known mobsters. Others might stake out the places where the criminals lived or worked. When the agents got enough information, they would raid the warehouses where large amounts of liquor were stored. After they arrested the bootleggers, the agents would take and destroy the liquor that was found.

Al Capone tried to have his men bribe these agents when they had become too successful. He was never able to get them to take money, though. One agent even chased down a gangster to return a large amount of cash that had been thrown in his car by one of Capone's men. Elliott Ness made sure this story got to the newspapers. Soon after that, the press nicknamed this special unit the Untouchables. They were "untouchable" because they could not be bribed or bullied.

The Untouchables seized large amounts of liquor and made many arrests. One man they could never arrest for liquor violations was Al Capone. However, they could show him that they were hurting his business. One night the agents paraded over forty trucks they had taken in raids, past Capone's hotel. The vehicles had been washed and polished until they were shiny and new-looking. Heavily armed agents accompanied the parade of trucks—in the front, the middle, and the rear. Capone's men rushed out of the hotel, but there was nothing they could do with all the police and special agents there. Al Capone was angry. He did not like this "parade." He wanted Elliott Ness killed, but the "hit" never took place.

While Al Capone was never convicted of bootlegging or murder, the agents had gathered a lot of information about his other activities. Finally, in 1931, Al Capone was convicted of income tax evasion. He was sentenced to eleven years in jail. The Untouchables moved on to other gangsters.

Glamour Begins to Fade

With the St. Valentine's Day Massacre, the glamorous image of the gangster began to fade. People did not mind illegal drinking, but they were fed up with gang violence, killings, and even government corruption.

Before passage of the Eighteenth Amendment, drys had argued that Prohibition would be good for the country. They said crime and violence would decrease if alcohol was prohibited. Now, the wets could point out that this had not happened. Instead, crime and corruption had increased with national Prohibition. The drys had also predicted that Americans' desire for alcohol would lessen, but this had not happened, either. In fact, the demand for alcohol had increased with Prohibition. Now, even those who had been in favor of Prohibition felt it was time to take a closer look at what was happening to the country. Many Americans thought it was time to consider repeal.

MOVEMENT TOWARD REPEAL

By the mid-1920s, the Anti-Saloon League and other drys were losing support. By 1926, many Americans already favored either repeal or modification of the Eighteenth Amendment.[1]

Members of the league wanted industrial alcohol to be made more poisonous so it would be harder to make it drinkable. Wayne Wheeler, president of the Anti-Saloon League, said, "The person who drinks this industrial alcohol is a deliberate suicide."[2] Many drys stopped supporting the league because they said Wheeler's suggestion, if followed, would amount to the government's trying to enforce the law by poisoning people.

The league lost rural support, too, as more and more people moved from the country to the city in order to find work. Then, Wayne Wheeler died suddenly of a heart attack in 1927. The loss of its major spokesperson hit the league hard. A few years later, Mabel Willebrandt resigned from the U.S. attorney's office to work for Fruit Industries, Inc., the makers of Vine-Glo. Willebrandt convinced Congress that although Vine-Glo fermented into wine with an alcoholic content of 12 percent, "Section 29 of the National Prohibition Act specifically permits you to have Vine-Glo in your home provided simply that you do not transport it or sell it."[3]

Thoughts About Repeal

Many Americans were convinced that Prohibition was creating more problems than it was solving. However, most felt there was little chance the Eighteenth Amendment could be repealed. An amendment had never been repealed. In fact, the Constitution had been written in such a way that it made repeal difficult. In order to repeal an amendment, another amendment had to be passed that would repeal the earlier amendment.

The presidential election of 1928 grew near. Herbert Hoover made it clear how he felt about Prohibition. "I do not favor the repeal of the 18th Amendment," he said. "I stand, of course, for the efficient, vigorous and sincere enforcement of the laws enacted thereunder. Whoever is chosen President has under his oath the solemn duty to pursue this course."

Hoover also said the United States had "deliberately undertaken a great social and economic experiment, noble in motive and far-reaching in purpose."[4] He thought this experiment should be worked out constructively.

Hoover's opponent, Al Smith, favored repeal of the Eighteenth Amendment, which mirrored the feeling of most of the nation. However, Smith lost the election mainly because he was an urban

Catholic candidate. At the time, many Americans were anti-Catholic and were not ready to elect a Catholic president.

The Wickersham Commission

In 1929, President Hoover created the National Commission on Law Observance and Law Enforcement. He appointed George W. Wickersham to head this commission, which became known as the Wickersham Commission. The purpose of the

---

SOURCE DOCUMENT

X—CONCLUSIONS AND RECOMMENDATIONS

1. THE COMMISSION IS OPPOSED TO REPEAL OF THE EIGHTEENTH AMENDMENT.

2. THE COMMISSION IS OPPOSED TO RESTORATION IN ANY MANNER OF THE LEGALIZED SALOON.

3. THE COMMISSION IS OPPOSED TO THE FEDERAL OR STATE GOVERNMENTS, AS SUCH, GOING INTO THE LIQUOR BUSINESS.

4. THE COMMISSION IS OPPOSED TO THE PROPOSAL TO MODIFY THE NATIONAL PROHIBITION ACT SO AS TO PERMIT MANUFACTURE AND SALE OF LIGHT WINES OR BEER. . . .

7. THE COMMISSION IS OF [THE] OPINION THAT THERE IS NO YET ADEQUATE OBSERVANCE OR ENFORCEMENT [OF THE LAW].[5]

The Wickersham Commission's report stated that the Eighteenth Amendment should not be repealed or made less strict. It instead indicated that the problem was not with the law, but with poor law enforcement.

Wickersham Commission was to make a thorough investigation of crime. In 1931, the Wickersham Commission made its final report. It concluded that the federal system for enforcing criminal law in the United States was not working. According to the commission, Prohibition enforcement had broken down.

Ten out of eleven commission members (though not Wickersham) signed a summary opposing repeal of the Eighteenth Amendment, the entry of the federal or state governments into the liquor business, and the modification of national Prohibition to permit the sale of light wines and beer.

The Jones Law

Hoover felt that stricter penalties would help enforce the Eighteenth Amendment. He was willing to see some revision of the amendment along these lines. The Jones Law, named after Senator Wesley L. Jones of Washington, who proposed it, amended the Volstead Act. It increased the penalties for breaking the law against alcohol. It raised the maximum penalties for first liquor offenses from six months in jail or a fine of a thousand dollars to a new maximum sentence of five years or ten thousand dollars, or both. Congress voted in favor of this change. It went into effect in March 1929.

Most Americans strongly opposed this change. They felt this was done merely in revenge, to get back at anyone who opposed Prohibition.

By 1929, prisons in America were overcrowded with people serving sentences for violating the Volstead Act. By this time, there had been over five hundred thousand arrests made in an attempt to enforce the act.[6] The courts were backlogged with Prohibition cases. Neither the local nor the federal government could effectively deal with this level of crime. Those who opposed Prohibition pointed out that the country's five federal penitentiaries were already overcrowded with prisoners who had violated the liquor law. To solve this problem, Hoover authorized the construction of six new federal prisons.

The Reformation Movement

There were many other organizations that opposed Prohibition in the 1920s. Among these were the National Association Opposed to Prohibition; the Moderation League; the American Veterans' Association for the Repeal of the Eighteenth Amendment; and the Women's Committee for Modification of the Volstead Act (which became the Women's Committee for Repeal of the Eighteenth Amendment). None of these were major organizations in the growing movement for reform, however. Instead, the Association Against the Prohibition Amendment (AAPA), the Crusaders, and the Women's Organization for National Prohibition Reform (WONPR) would be the three most important organizations in the reformation movement.

The Association Against the Prohibition Amendment (AAPA)

The AAPA had been founded by Captain William H. Stayton in 1918, as World War I ended. Stayton said that "the Constitution is no place for prohibition. That is a local question."[7]

Stayton signed up friends from his navy days to start the organization. It was not long before wealthy businessmen from all areas of the country joined the association, too. Although the organization's efforts were too late to stop the ratification of the Eighteenth Amendment, members of the AAPA continued to express opposition to it.

Throughout Prohibition, Stayton often spoke out about it before large crowds. At a speech in New York City's Carnegie Hall in 1922, Stayton said the Eighteenth Amendment was "a rotten insult to the American people" and a law that said Americans could not be trusted. He added, "this prohibition business is only a symptom of a disease, the desire of fanatics to meddle in the other man's affairs and to regulate the details of your lives and mine."[8]

The AAPA was in favor of temperance. Stayton and other members of the AAPA felt that forcing Prohibition through a constitutional law would create intemperance. In the early 1920s, the AAPA worked to ease the restrictions of the Volstead Act since repeal would be so difficult. Members of the AAPA all wanted Prohibition reformed "in such a way as to guarantee against the return of the saloon."[9]

Congressional hearings on modifying the Volstead Act were held in April and May of 1924. Groups that opposed Prohibition wanted the law modified so beer containing 2.75 percent alcohol would be legal. Hugh Fox of the U.S. Brewers' Association claimed that this beer would be the "salvation of the prohibition experiment."[10] Fox predicted that legal beer would undermine the bootlegging business and lead to much greater compliance with the Prohibition laws.

Prohibitionists did not want modifications made in the law. They called for more effective enforcement of the Volstead Act. They refused to compromise, and since they still had much political influence, the Volstead Act was not modified.

In 1930, Senator Morris Sheppard of Texas, who had helped write the Eighteenth Amendment, claimed, "There is as much chance of repealing the Eighteenth Amendment as there is for a hummingbird to fly to the planet Mars with the Washington Monument tied to its tail."[11]

The Women's Organization for National Prohibition Reform (WONPR)

Just as women organized before the Eighteenth Amendment in favor of Prohibition, now women organized to oppose Prohibition and promote repeal. Drys assumed women would still be in favor of Prohibition, but they were wrong. Women could prove that they had some real political power now.

President Hebert Hoover was not in favor of repealing the Eighteenth Amendment. Instead, he favored stricter federal enforcement of the Prohibition laws.

Pauline Sabin was the wife of a prominent banker, Charles H. Sabin, treasurer of the AAPA. She was also the first woman member of the Republican National Committee. Sabin said she favored Prohibition in theory, but was now convinced that it was a failure. Prohibition was supposed to help children, but that had not happened. Drunkenness among children and teenagers had increased greatly. Saloons were gone, but they had been replaced by thousands of speakeasies. Although she had worked hard to get Herbert Hoover elected, Sabin was upset with President Hoover's inauguration speech in which he promised to take a harder stand against alcohol. When Congress passed the Jones Act in 1929, Sabin resigned from the Republican National Committee. She created the WONPR. She launched this new organization at the Drake Hotel in Chicago. In its declaration of principles, the organization stated that Prohibition was "disastrous in consequences in the hypocrisy, the corruption, the tragic loss of life and the appalling increase of crime which have attended the abortive attempt to enforce it."[12]

The WONPR was very popular right from the start. Soon it had a million members. Each local chapter of this organization was led by a woman with her own income who had an impressive place in society. These women attracted middle-class women to the organization. It soon became fashionable to oppose Prohibition.

The Crusaders

The third organization that opposed Prohibition was called the Crusaders. This group began in Cleveland, Ohio, the same state where the Anti-Saloon League started. The Crusaders concentrated on local politics instead of national government. Fred G. Clark was the first leader of the Crusaders. Mr. Clark was an oil executive in Cleveland.

The Crusaders wanted temperance and the elimination of the corrupt politicians and other officials that Prohibition had created.

Cultural Attitudes and the Great Depression

By the late 1920s, cultural attitudes toward drinking had also started to change. Saloons had appealed to immigrants and the lower class, which offended the middle class. Saloons were replaced by speakeasies. Speakeasies were middle-class drinking establishments and therefore were more acceptable to the general population.

The late 1920s was a difficult economic time for Americans. In 1929, the stock market crashed. The value of stock on the market went down a large amount in a short period of time. People who had invested in the stock market lost money because they were selling their stock shares at much lower prices than they had paid for them. People and companies who had invested large amounts in the stock market were now bankrupt or deeply in debt. Businesses failed. Banks closed. Millions of people lost their jobs and their savings and could not afford to pay their bills. Soon, they were more concerned with finding work and feeding their families than with solving the problems of Prohibition.

Americans kept drinking, and the government kept trying to enforce the Volstead Act. Yet, police could not keep up with the illegal liquor business. There were simply too many people involved—everyone from doctors and druggists who prescribed and filled false prescriptions for medicinal alcohol to bootleggers, speakeasy operators, and gangsters. To make matters worse, much of the country was experiencing long periods of drought. This caused crops to fail, so many farmers went bankrupt. By 1932, more than 12 million Americans were out of work. It was perhaps the bleakest period in American history. People did what they could to survive. This often meant bootlegging and rumrunning.

By 1932, President Hoover did not have much of a chance for reelection. Presidents are rarely reelected in a time of economic downturn. Americans lost confidence in this president who had promised that the economy would get better quickly. People began to resent Hoover for concentrating on enforcing Prohibition, rather than facing the facts of the country's economic disaster. Enforcing Prohibition seemed silly in light of everyone's more immediate problems.

The drys had promised life would be better with Prohibition. There would be less crime, more prosperity, and less violence. None of these promises came true. Now, the wets pointed out that life would be better without Prohibition. The government was not collecting large amounts in taxes on liquor. Instead, gangsters were gaining all the profits. Government was not making money on alcohol; it was spending money trying to enforce the unenforceable Volstead Act. Repealing Prohibition would restore jobs and tax dollars.

THE
END OF
PROHIBITION

The AAPA was set up much like the Anti-Saloon League that had helped to bring about national alcohol prohibition in 1920. The method of both the Anti-Saloon League and the AAPA was to actively promote those candidates for public office who favored their position.

Drys thought that since women had led the fight for Prohibition, they would continue their support. To drys, this meant women would "vote dry" now that they had the right to vote. Women as a whole, however, had changed since the days before Prohibition. In the 1800s and early 1900s, women did not visit saloons or drink in public places very often. Now women enjoyed speakeasies just as men did. In 1932, newspaper and magazine surveys showed that an increasing majority of men and women favored either modification or outright repeal of the Volstead Act.

By this time, people had seen for themselves that Prohibition could not be enforced. Even though the prisons were being filled and more had to be built, there were many more bootleggers and speakeasies still in operation. Some corrupt police and public officials were taking bribes to ignore illegal liquor sales. With no government regulations to monitor the liquor that consumers were getting, the quality of the liquor available could vary greatly. Sometimes it was deadly, as when poisonous industrial alcohol was mistaken for the drinkable kind. The government was also losing potential revenue from the taxation and regulation of alcoholic beverages. None of this seemed to make sense.

Opponents of Prohibition now included some of the most respectable men and women in the country. Influential businessmen like millionaire Pierre S. DuPont argued that if liquor were legal and could be taxed, the government would receive enough money to quickly pay off the national debt. John D. Rockefeller, Jr., another wealthy businessman, had been in favor of Prohibition and a dry all his life. He, like William Randolph Hearst, the publishing tycoon, had worked for the passage of the Eighteenth Amendment. However, in the late 1920s, Rockefeller joined the wets to repeal Prohibition. With these wealthy businessmen, the reason for such a change of heart was purely business, though they did not always make it sound that way. They knew they would be paying more and more taxes to enforce the Volstead Act. They did not like the thought of that.

The 1932 Presidential Election

President Herbert Hoover was running for reelection. He had already made his views on Prohibition known.

He was firmly against repeal when he accepted the Republication nomination again. Everyone knew that he had spent a great deal of time and effort during his past administration trying to enforce Prohibition. However, he changed his opinion on this issue right before the 1932 election. Hoover said he now felt that liquor regulation should be put under state control. This made dry supporters angry. Hoover lost many of his past supporters, yet did not gain many new ones, as most wets favored Roosevelt.

Franklin Delano Roosevelt was the Democratic party's nominee for president. During the presidential campaign, the big issue was the Depression, not Prohibition. Most people felt Roosevelt was the man to help change the country's economic situation. Millions of Americans were without money or jobs, and crime and corruption still plagued the nation. Roosevelt had avoided any position on repeal, however. Then, he endorsed repeal in his acceptance speech for the Democratic nomination when he said:

> I congratulate this convention for having had the courage, fearlessly, to write into its declaration of principles what an overwhelming majority here assembled really thinks about the Eighteenth Amendment. This convention wants repeal. Your candidate wants repeal. And I am confident that the United States of America wants repeal.[1]

In the end, Roosevelt won the election.

The Twenty-first Amendment

Many politicians wanted to vote for repeal, but they were hesitant to change their minds and upset their supporters. Luckily, the Constitution provides two ways to propose amendments and two ways to ratify them. Once an amendment has been proposed, it can be ratified by either state legislatures or by special state ratification conventions. Congressmen could choose the conventions method and not look as if they were changing their minds. After all, they would not be voting for repeal. They would be voting to let the people decide for themselves what they wanted to do

SOURCE DOCUMENT

Section 1.

THE EIGHTEENTH ARTICLE OF AMENDMENT TO THE CONSTITUTION OF THE UNITED STATES IS HEREBY REPEALED.

Section 2.

THE TRANSPORTATION OR IMPORTATION INTO ANY STATE, TERRITORY, OR POSSESSION OF THE UNITED STATES FOR DELIVERY OR USE THEREIN OF INTOXICATING LIQUORS, IN VIOLATION OF THE LAWS THEREOF, IS HEREBY PROHIBITED.

Section 3.

THIS ARTICLE SHALL BE INOPERATIVE UNLESS IT SHALL HAVE BEEN RATIFIED AS AN AMENDMENT TO THE CONSTITUTION BY CONVENTIONS IN THE SEVERAL STATES, AS PROVIDED IN THE CONSTITUTION, WITHIN SEVEN YEARS FROM THE DATE OF THE SUBMISSION HEREOF TO THE STATES BY CONGRESS.[2]

Ratified on December 5, 1933, the Twenty-first Amendment ended the Prohibition era.

about Prohibition. Special elections were held where communities voted by secret ballot to send either a wet or dry delegate. This meant state legislators did not have to worry, either.

On December 6, 1932, a congressional resolution was drafted. It called for the repeal of the Eighteenth Amendment. The necessary two thirds of both the Senate and the House of Representatives approved the resolution on February 16, 1933.

After Congress approved the repeal resolution, it was sent to the states for ratification. Thirty-six, or three fourths, of the states had to ratify it. On December 5, 1933, Utah became the thirty-sixth state to do so, and the resolution was ratified as the Twenty-first Amendment to the Constitution. At 7:00 P.M., Roosevelt signed the proclamation that ended America's "Noble Experiment." It had lasted thirteen years, ten months, and eighteen days.

Some states chose to remain dry for a while after repeal of the Eighteenth Amendment. Kansas was dry until 1948, Oklahoma until 1957, and Mississippi until 1966.

The Beer Bill

When Roosevelt took office, he proposed that Congress immediately modify the Volstead Act to allow light wines and beer to be sold. In April 1933, the U.S. Congress passed the Cullen-Harrison Act declaring that beer with a 3.2 percent alcohol content was not intoxicating and could be sold. This beer, almost as strong as regular beer, was now legal.

Celebrations

Americans celebrated right away, even though the president of the U.S. Brewers' Association advised against "untoward celebration,"[3] meaning that people should not go out and get drunk. The Anheuser-Busch Brewery in St. Louis delivered beer to area taverns. In Milwaukee, people waited outside the breweries to buy beer, receive a free glass of beer, or apply for new jobs at the breweries. Across the country, people drank a million and a half barrels of beer the first day beer was made legal again. The next day, there was a nationwide beer shortage.

Just as Prohibitionists had held mock funerals for John Barleycorn when Prohibition started, now people burned straw-packed dummies labeled Prohibition to symbolize the death of the Eighteenth Amendment.

9

A LOOK
BACK

Before the Eighteenth Amendment took effect in 1920, Prohibitionists said passage of this amendment would help solve the nation's problems. Poverty, health problems, and crime would all get better since these were supposedly the result of alcohol consumption. According to the Prohibitionists, alcohol created sickness and disease. If people gave it up, they would be healthier. They would get better jobs. Productivity would increase and absenteeism would decrease throughout offices, factories, and other workplaces throughout the country. Crime would disappear. The government would have more money because prisons and poorhouses would be empty.

The Wickersham Commission concluded that the country had Prohibition only in theory, not in fact. It reported:

> "There was general prevalence of drinking in homes, in clubs and in hotels" . . . Throughout the country, "people of wealth, businessmen and professional men, and their families, and . . . the higher paid working-men and their families, are drinking in large numbers" in openly flouting [disregarding] of the law. And

After the Twenty-first Amendment was ratified, President Franklin D. Roosevelt signed the official proclamation that ended Prohibition.

neither Congress nor the states set up adequate machinery or appropriated sufficient funds for the enforcement of the prohibitory legislation.[1]

As the United States found out, Prohibition just creates new problems.

Fewer Jobs

Many people who had legally worked in the liquor trade were suddenly without a way to earn a living when the Volstead Act went into effect. Owners of breweries, distilleries, and wineries, for example, had to figure out a new way to use these factories, or they had to find other work. People who had worked for them needed to find new jobs, too, if these breweries, distilleries, and wineries could not be used in other ways.

Some Americans were worse off than ever. They had to find some way to make a living, so they went back to the only thing they knew—alcohol. This made them criminals, and soon many were ignoring the law because it did not seem like a crime to do something that had once been legal.

More Crime

There were ten homicides for every one hundred thousand people during the 1920s. This was a 78 percent increase over the pre-Prohibition period. Also, with the passage of the Volstead Act, the number of crimes increased 24 percent between 1920 and 1921. By 1932, the number of federal convicts had increased 561 percent, to 26,589. The federal prison population had increased 366 percent. Much of this increase was due to violations of the Volstead Act. Convictions for Prohibition violations increased 1,000 percent between 1925 and 1930. This dramatic increase in the prison population led to more spending on prisons and severe overcrowding.[2]

Not only was there more crime in general during Prohibition, but there was a rise in organized crime as well. Organizations committed serious crimes while defending their sales territories, brand names, and labor contracts. Organized crime did not end with repeal. When alcohol sales became legal once again, wealthy gangsters moved on to other businesses, including the illegal drug trade.

By the early 1930s, the country did not have less crime. It had more. This meant the government was now worse off, too. Prisons did not empty. As they filled to capacity, more prisons had to be built.

Less Revenue but More Expenses

The government also took in less money during Prohibition, yet it had to spend more and more. No money could be collected from taxes on alcohol, but millions of dollars were needed to enforce the Volstead Act. The Prohibition Bureau originally had an annual budget of $4.4 million. This jumped to $13.4 million during the 1920s. Coast Guard spending on Prohibition averaged over $13 million per year. There were also state and local government expenses for enforcement of the liquor laws.

More Danger

During Prohibition, alcohol became more potent. Often it was made with dangerous substances. The typical Prohibition beer, wine, or whiskey contained a higher percentage of alcohol by volume than that produced before or after Prohibition. It is estimated that the potency of Prohibition-era products was 150 percent higher than the potency of products produced either before or after Prohibition.[3]

Changed Habits

Prohibition was supposed to change America's drinking habits, but not in the way that it did. Prohibitionists said people would get used to drinking less. Instead, alcohol became more attractive to young people because it was a product they associated with excitement and intrigue. Also, many Americans were unwilling to be told that they could not drink. As a result, "Men were drinking defiantly, with a sense of high purpose, a kind of dedicated drinking that you don't see much of today," according to author Henry Lee.[4]

During Prohibition, speakeasies were everywhere, so people were still drinking. People also drank more patent medicines (which contained high concentrations of alcohol). They also drank more medicinal alcohol and sacramental alcohol during this time. Physicians and hospitals doubled the alcoholic liquors they sold between 1923 and 1931. The amount of medicinal alcohol (95 percent pure alcohol) sold increased by 400 percent.

Prohibitionists assumed that if people could not spend their money on alcohol, they would use it for other things like modern appliances, savings, and education. But people did not spend less on alcohol. They spent more. They also bought more substitutes for alcohol, such as tobacco and dangerous drugs.

Effects of Repeal

The Great Depression did not end with the Twenty-first Amendment, as many people had hoped. Joblessness and hunger continued to be major problems until the early 1940s. When the country prepared for World War II, the economy improved.

Repeal of Prohibition did dramatically reduce crime, including organized crime and corruption. Also, jobs were created.

Americans changed the way they thought about drinking. Instead of considering drinking to be a political issue, more people saw it as a personal issue. They felt that most adults could drink responsibly. Those who could not needed help and treatment, not laws. For the first time, new voluntary groups, such as Alcoholics Anonymous, which was started in 1934, provided help for alcoholics.

A Lesson Learned

Moralists and social reformers believed that passage of the Eighteenth Amendment would be enough to change the habits of American society as a whole. They were wrong. This did not happen. But repeal did not solve the nation's alcohol problem, either. In fact, alcoholism is still a major social problem in the United States today. And, there are still restrictions on alcohol use, although most of these restrictions are decided at the state or local level rather than by the federal government. Still, in the early 1980s, the federal government withheld funds to some states, forcing them to raise their drinking age to twenty-one.

A report in a 1994 issue of the *Journal of the American Medical Association* said, "Alcohol contributes to 100,000 deaths annually, making it the third leading cause of preventable mortality in the US, after tobacco and diet/activity patterns."[5]

Today, coalitions like the National Commission Against Drunk Driving (NCADD) exist to help deal with drunk driving, one of the nation's biggest health and public safety problems.

Neither national Prohibition nor repeal solved America's alcohol problem. Instead, the nation learned what can happen when too many restrictions are placed on the American public. It is likely that alcohol use will remain a topic of public policy debate and government action for quite some time.

★ TIMELINE ★

1607—Jamestown, Virginia, becomes the first permanent English settlement in the New World; Aqua vitae (an alcoholic beverage) is part of each colonist's supplies.

1630—Puritans bring alcohol to the Massachusetts Bay Colony.

1633—Plymouth Colony limits the sale of spirits.

1785—Dr. Benjamin Rush publishes a pamphlet about the effects of spirituous liquors on the body and mind.

1813—Massachusetts Society for the Suppression of Intemperance (MSSI) is started.

1826—Reverend Lyman Beecher delivers six sermons on the dangers of drinking.

1840—The Washingtonians, a temperance society, is formed.

1851—Maine passes the first state Prohibition law.

1861—The Civil War begins, which diverts people's attention from alcohol issues.

1864—President Abraham Lincoln signs the Internal Revenue Act, which places a tax on the manufacture of liquor and beer and charges a fee to all retail liquor establishments in an effort to raise money for the war.

1869—The National Prohibition party is formed.

1874—The Women's Christian Temperance Union (WCTU) is established.

1881—Kansas becomes first state to make Prohibition part of its state constitution.

1893—The Anti-Saloon League is organized.

1899—Carry Nation begins a series of raids on saloons across the country.

1917—*April 6*: America enters World War I.

December 18: Congress passes the Eighteenth Amendment to the Constitution.

1919—*January 16*: The Eighteenth Amendment is ratified by the states.

October 28: The Volstead Act is passed.

1920—Prohibition begins.

1929—*February 14*: St. Valentine's Day Massacre.

October 24: Stock market crashes.

1931—Wickersham Commission delivers its final report.

1932—The Twenty-first Amendment is introduced in Congress.

1933—*February 16*: Twenty-first Amendment is approved by Congress.

December 5: Prohibition ends.

★ CHAPTER NOTES ★

Chapter 1. America Says "No" to Alcohol

1. "Eighteenth Amendment—Prohibition of Intoxicating Liquors," *The Constitution of the United States of America,* November 1, 1996, <http://www.access.gpo.gov/congress/senate/constitution/amdt18.html> (May 28, 2002).

2. John Kobler, *Ardent Spirits: The Rise and Fall of Prohibition* (New York: G.P. Putnam's Sons, 1973), p. 11.

3. Ibid., p. 12.

4. David E. Kyvig, *Repealing National Prohibition* (The University of Chicago Press, 1979), p. 19.

5. "Act of October 28, 1919 (Volstead Act)," *The Volstead Act and Related Prohibition Documents*, n.d., <http://media.nara.gov/media/images/19/28/19-2762a.jpg> (May 28, 2002).

6. Kobler, p. 13.

7. Ibid.

Chapter 2. The History of Alcohol and the Brewing Industry

1. "Letter received by Banks from N. Hulme, August 1, 1768, (Series 03.229)," *Endeavour Journal*, n.d. <http://www.slnsw.gov.au/Banks/series_03/03_229.htm> (January 2002).

2. Thomas R. Pegram, *Battling Demon Rum: The Struggle for a Dry America, 1800–1933* (Chicago: Ivan R. Dee, 1998), p. 7.

3. Ernest H. Cherrington, *The Evolution of Prohibition in the United States of America* (Ohio: American Issue Press, 1920), p. 18.

4. Pegram, p. 7.

5. John Kobler, *Ardent Spirits: The Rise and Fall of Prohibition* (New York: G.P. Putnam's Sons, 1973), p. 33.

6. Ibid., p. 37.

7. Ibid., p. 30.

8. Bill Severn, *The End of the Roaring Twenties: Prohibition and Repeal* (New York: Julian Messner, 1969), p. 23.

9. Kobler, p. 25.

10. Norman H. Clark, *Deliver Us From Evil* (New York: W.W. Norton & Company, 1976), p. 19.

11. Kobler, p. 30.

12. W. J. Rorabaugh, *The Alcoholic Republic: An American Tradition* (New York: Oxford University Press, 1979), pp. 8–9.

13. Pegram, pp. 92–93.

14. Larry Engelmann, *Intemperance, The Lost War Against Liquor* (New York: The Free Press, 1979), p. 3.

15. "The Saloon in an Illinois Coal-Mining Town," Missionary Review, 1902, <http://www.history.ohio-state.edu/projects/prohibition/saloons/SaloonsCoalIl> (March 2001).

16. George Kibbe Turner, "The City of Chicago, A Study of the Great Immoralitites," *McClure's Magazine,* April 1907, pp. 576–579.

17. Engelmann, p. 4.

18. Clark, p. 2.

19. Engelmann, p. 7.

Chapter 3. Temperance Groups

1. Ernest H. Cherrington, *The Evolution of Prohibition in the United States of America* (Ohio: American Issue Press, 1920), p. 37.

2. Edward Behr, *Prohibition: Thirteen Years that Changed America* (New York: Arcade Publishing, 1996), p. 23.

3. Ibid., p. 24.

4. A.W. Chase, "A Temperance Pledge," *Victorian Household Elegance,* January 2002, <http://www.victorianlinks.com/elegancies/02/01/pledge.shtml> (May 28, 2002).

5. J. C. Furnas, *The Life and Times of the Late Demon Rum* (New York: G.P. Putnam's Sons, 1965), p. 167.

6. "The Woman's Crusade in Xenia, Ohio," n.d., <http://www.history.ohio-state.edu/projects/prohibition/xenia.htm> (March 2001).

7. Furnas, p. 281.

8. Peter H. Odegard, *Pressure Politics—The Story of the Antisaloon League* (New York: Columbia University Press, 1928), pp. 40–59.

9. Larry Engelmann, *Intemperance, The Lost War Against Liquor* (New York: The Free Press, 1979), p. 11.

10. "History of the Anti-Saloon League 1893–1933," n.d., <http://www.wpl.lib.oh.us/AntiSaloon/history> (March 2001).

11. Carolyn E.Geisel, *Speeches of the Flying Squadron* (Indianapolis: Hanley and Stewart, 1915), pp. 415–416.

12. Andrew Sinclair, *Prohibition: The Era of Excess* (Boston: Little, Brown, 1962), p. 122.

Chapter 4. The Roaring Twenties

1. Kelley Kawano, "F. Scott Fitzgerald," *Bold Type* magazine, n.d. <http://www.randomhouse.com/boldtype/1101/fitzgerald/> (February 22, 2002).

2. Sean Dennis Cashman, *Prohibition: The Lie of the Land* (New York: The Free Press, 1981), p. 53.

3. "Society, Fads, Daily Life," *The 1920s*, March 26, 2000 <http://www.louisville.edu/~kprayb01/1920s-Society-1.html#B> (August 2001).

4. Marc McCutcheon, *The Writer's Guide to Everyday Life from Prohibition through World War II* (Cincinnati, Ohio: Writer's Digest Books, 1995), p. 24.

Chapter 5. Illegal Liquor

1. Thomas M. Coffey, *The Long Thirst, Prohibition in America: 1920–1933* (New York: W.W. Norton & Company, Inc., 1975), p. 265.

2. Norman H. Clark, *Deliver Us from Evil* (New York: W.W. Norton & Company, 1976), p. 159.

3. Sean Dennis Cashman, *Prohibition: The Lie of the Land* (New York: The Free Press, 1981), p. 168.

4. "Society, Fads, Daily Life," *The 1920s*, March 26, 2000, <http://www.louisville.edu/~kprayb01/1920s-Society-2.html#A=1> (February 2001).

5. "Alcohol Prohibition Was a Failure," *Policy Analysis*, July 17, 1991, <http://www.cato.org/pubs/pas/pa-157.html> (March 2001).

6. Edward Behr, *Prohibition: Thirteen Years that Changed America* (New York: Arcade Publishing, 1996), p. 221.

7. John Kobler, *Ardent Spirits: The Rise and Fall of Prohibition* (New York: G.P. Putnam's Sons, 1973), p. 224.

Chapter 6. The Growth of Organized Crime

1. Edward Behr, *Prohibition: Thirteen Years that Changed America* (New York: Arcade Publishing, 1996), p. 177.

2. "Prohibition Movement," n.d. <http://www.tdstelme.net/~jwalker/movement.htm> (January 2001).

3. "Al Capone: St. Valentine's Day," *The Crime Library* © 2001, <http://www.crimelibrary.com/capone/caponesaint.htm> (March 2001).

4. "The St. Valentine's Day Massacre," *InfoPlease* © 2000–2002, <http://www.infoplease.com/spot/valmassacre1.html> (March 2001).

Chapter 7. Movement Toward Repeal

1. Edward Behr, *Prohibition: Thirteen Years that Changed America* (New York: Arcade Publishing, 1996), p. 221.

2. Ibid., p. 222.

3. John Kobler, *Ardent Spirits: The Rise and Fall of Prohibition* (New York: G.P. Putnam's Sons, 1973), p. 347.

4. Norman H. Clark, *Deliver Us from Evil* (New York: W.W. Norton & Company, 1976), p. 191.

5. "X–Conclusions and Recommendations," *Wickersham Commission Report on Alcohol Prohibition*, n.d., <http://www.druglibrary.org/schaffer/Library/studies/wick/wick10.html> (May 28, 2002).

6. "Volstead Act Statistics," *Shaffer Library of Drug Policy*, December 1930, <http://www.druglibrary.org/schaffer/library/graphs/volstead9.htm> (February 2001).

7. David E. Kyvig, *Repealing National Prohibition* (Chicago: The University of Chicago Press, 1979), p. 43.

8. Ibid., p. 50.

9. Sean Dennis Cashman, *Prohibition: The Lie of the Land* (New York: The Free Press, 1981), p. 158.

10. Larry Engelmann, *Intemperance, The Lost War Against Liquor* (New York: The Free Press, 1979), p. 189.

11. Ibid.

12. "Chapter 7—Hard Times, Hopeful Times," *Repealing National Prohibition*, 1979, (Schaffer Library of Drug Policy), <http://www.druglibrary.org/schaffer/history/rnp/RNP7.html> (February 2001).

Chapter 8. The End of Prohibition

1. Fletcher Dobyns, *The Amazing Story of Repeal* (Evanston, Ill.: Signal Press, 1965), p. 160.

2. "Twenty-First Amendment—Repeal of Eighteenth Amendment," The Constitution of the United States of America, November 1, 1996, <http://www.access.gpo.gov/congress/senate/constitution/amdt21.html> (May 28, 2002).

3. John Kobler, *Ardent Spirits: The Rise and Fall of Prohibition* (New York: G.P. Putnam's Sons, 1973), p. 352.

Chapter 9. A Look Back

1. Tun Yuan Hu, *The Liquor Tax in the United States: 1791–1947* (New York: Columbia University Press, 1950), p. 52.

2. "Alcohol Prohibition Was a Failure," *Policy Analysis,* July 17, 1991, <http://www.cato.org/pubs/pas/pa-157.html> (March 2001).

3. Ibid.

4. Ibid.

5. J. McGinnis and W. Foege, "Actual Cause of Death in the United States," *Journal of the American Medical Association*, vol. 270, no. 18 (November 10, 1993), p. 2208.

★ FURTHER READING ★

Altman, Linda Jacobs. *The Decade That Roared: America During Prohibition.* New York: Twentieth Century Books, 1997.

Feinstein, Stephen. *The 1920s from Prohibition to Charles Lindbergh.* Berkeley Heights, N.J.: Enslow Publishers, 2001.

Hinman, Bonnie. *The Bootlegger Menace.* Uhrichsville, Ohio: Barbour & Co., 1998.

King, David C. *Al Capone and the Roaring Twenties.* Woodbridge, Conn.: Blackbirch Press, 1999.

King, David C. *The Roaring Twenties.* Carlisle, Mass.: Discovery Enterprises, Ltd., 1997.

Lucas, Eileen. *The Eighteenth and Twenty-First Amendments— Alcohol—Prohibition and Repeal.* Springfield, N.J.: Enslow Publishers, 1998.

Rebman, Renee C. *Prohibition.* San Diego: Lucent Books, 1999.

★ INTERNET ADDRESSES ★

The Constitution of the United States of America. *Eighteenth Amendment—Prohibition of Intoxicating Liquors.* November 1, 1996. <http://www.access.gpo.gov/congress/senate/constitution/amdt18.html>.

The Ohio State University Department of History. *Temperance & Prohibition.* © 1997. <http://prohibition.history.ohio-state.edu/>.

Westerville Public Library. *The Anti-Saloon League 1893–1933.* n.d. <http://www.wpl.lib.oh.us/AntiSaloon/>.

★ INDEX ★